☆

The human experience of the American Revolution—conveyed through contemporary letters, diaries, newspapers, and songs—that is what this book is about. "I endured hardships sufficient to kill a dozen horses . . . our men were cut up like cornstalks," wrote one young revolutionary stationed with General Washington in Delaware in 1777. For him, the Revolution was as real and bitterly difficult as the struggles taking place all over the world today protesting colonial exploitation. In the British enclaves the military could be heard toasting "the King, the Queen . . . the Ladies." But an English lieutenant tells us simply that "as the troops could not get their tents ashore from the transports, they were obliged to lie without any shelter, on a bleak hill."

The Living History Library is a new series, under the general editorship of John Anthony Scott, that provides a fresh and challenging approach to the study of the American past. Its overall theme as a series is the history of the United States as told by the people who shaped it. In each book, songs and documents of the period are joined by a sustaining commentary to illuminate a given facet or topic in the history of the American people.

The Living History Library

General editor: John Anthony Scott

Trumpet of a Prophecy

REVOLUTIONARY AMERICA

☆ *1763-1783* ☆

John Anthony Scott

Illustrated with maps and contemporary prints

ALFRED A. KNOPF : NEW YORK

973.3078

For Robin

INTRODUCTION

A revolution is no ordinary event in man's history. It is a time when life ceases to flow quietly and rises up in a violent flood that sweeps away people and familiar landmarks, and leaves the world a very different place when the storm subsides. Many revolutions have taken place among the peoples of the world in fairly recent times, but to the American people goes the honor of making one of the first *successful* revolutions of the modern era. This revolution lies at the very gateway of our history; it is a key to the understanding of our origins as a nation and to the shaping of a vision of our future. The high tide of the movement lasted for about twenty years, roughly from 1763 to 1783. It started with popular demonstrations, riots, and revolts; these led, in the course of time, to military confrontation, guerrilla warfare, and the violent overthrow of the established British government. When the bloodshed was over, Great Britain's American colonies were gone; in their place the United States of America had come into being as a separate and independent nation.

Important though the American Revolution may be

as a key to our own society and its future, it has an even wider significance: its study is relevant for the understanding of our entire planet today, the meaning of the struggles in which the earth's peoples are engaged, the agonies that they endure, and the destiny toward which they so painfully move. Americans were revolutionary pioneers: they undertook the first successful struggle in the modern world against a colonial empire that claimed the right to rule them for purposes not their own. From that day to this many other peoples have followed the American example. During the nineteenth century Latin American and Caribbean peoples cast aside their dependency on Portugal, France, and Spain. They continue to struggle to this very day against military intervention and other forms of control that have been imposed upon them. In the twentieth century many African and Asian peoples have joined the struggle against colonial rule. They have set the torch to the imperial rule and exploitation established by their British, French, Dutch, German, Italian, or Japanese overlords.

This struggle for freedom and independence is worldwide, it is far from over, and will continue for many years. Our own revolution can help us understand what is now going on throughout the globe: it not only illuminates our own destiny as a free people, but reveals to us why others will give everything they have, including life itself, for freedom. Our revolution helps us grasp the shape of the future that we and our children are to live in, if we are to survive at all—a future in which the family of man is divided not into rulers and ruled but only into communities of free, equal, and independent peoples.

CONTENTS

Introduction

Songs, Ballads, and Verse

Maps

SONGS, BALLADS, AND VERSE

MAPS

Trumpet of a Prophecy

THE LAND OF THE GRASSHOPPERS
British America in the Revolutionary Era

There is a pleasant landscape that lieth far away,
Beyond the wide Atlantic in North America.

Peter St. John of Norwalk, "American Taxation"

What was British America like, and what were its people like, during the fateful revolutionary period that stretched from 1763 to 1783?

In 1763 British America was a huge area bounded by the Atlantic Ocean on the east and the Mississippi River on the west, by the Great Lakes and the Gulf of St. Lawrence on the north, and by the Gulf of Mexico and Spanish Florida on the south. That very year, as a matter of fact, the size of Britain's American empire had been doubled by the conquest and seizure from France of her Canadian territory and the great interior valley of the Mississippi.

The thirteen American colonies were at that time the very heart and foundation of Britain's North American empire. In 1763 one hundred and fifty years of continuous organized settlement lay in back of these colonies.

British planters and immigrants, some of them aided by white bondservants and black slaves, had performed the remarkable feat of clearing and settling the coastal plain from the forests of Maine to the wilds of Georgia. By 1763, it is true, these settlers and pioneers had not yet penetrated the mighty stone ramparts of the Appalachian range, which hemmed them in between the mountains and the sea and blocked their advance into the interior; but even so, the land they had made their own was by any standards a vast one. It boasted broad forests and fertile fields; its shores teemed with fish, and its silver streams ran unpolluted to the sea.

The people who inhabited this American land were few in number and thinly scattered. The population in 1763 numbered not much more than 2.5 million souls, of whom one-half million, or about 20 percent, were slaves. The population, to be sure, was increasing rapidly: in 1790, when the first federal census was taken, it had grown to nearly 4 million.

The tiny population combined with the large area tells us something significant: British America was in fact what we today would call an underdeveloped country. It had infinite resources, but these still awaited exploitation. The overwhelming majority of the people—perhaps as much as 95 percent of them—were country dwellers: farmers, fisherfolk, and woodsmen who lived in moderate circumstances or outright poverty, and who survived only at the price of constant, unremitting labor. In the economy of the empire the colonies fulfilled (for the most part) their allotted role of providing raw or semi-finished materials—furs, rice, indigo, tobacco, ship supplies, lumber, and oil—for use or sale by Great Britain. They received in return all kinds of manufactured goods from the mother country, including clothing, cast-iron kettles, carpenter's tools, glass, clocks, and books.

There were a number of towns and cities in America where trade was conducted and the manufacture of goods was carried on, but these centers bore absolutely no resemblance to the modern industrial and commercial mazes in which most of us now live. They were not huge metropolitan areas engulfing millions of human beings, clamorous with rushing people and the racket of machines, belching smoke and fumes into a sooty atmosphere. With the exception of the three biggest (Philadelphia, New York, and Boston), all the colonial towns were no more than overgrown villages. In 1763 only twenty-five places in the entire country had more than 3,000 inhabitants; these were located, almost without exception, on the seacoasts and at the mouths of navigable rivers. No more than 5 percent of the people lived in these towns.

The town dwellers were merchants who made their money as middlemen in the import and export business; seamen who sailed the ships that moved raw materials from America to Europe, and manufactured goods in the reverse direction, who loaded and unloaded vessels at the docks, or who went hunting on the high seas after cod and whale. Or they were craftsmen, and their apprentices, who built ships, countinghouses, and townhouses for the merchants and planters; who manufactured rope, barrels, and ship's gear; who built chairs and other furniture; or who set type and published newspapers. Even Philadelphia, America's capital and its most thriving commercial center, boasted only 24,000 people in 1763; Manhattan, second most populous town, had 18,000; Boston, which came third, 16,000.

An eloquent picture of America at the time of the Revolution has been left us by J. Hector St. John Crevecoeur. Crevecoeur was born in the French province of Normandy in 1731; he emigrated from Europe in 1754, married an American wife, and settled down in the New World. He delighted in the luxuriant beauty of the wilderness, observed its wildlife with the devotion of a naturalist, and recorded it with the eye and pen of a poet. Crevecoeur felt that the air he breathed here was free; he did not find in British America the extremes of oppression, poverty, and class hatred that he had seen in feudal Europe. His gracious and beautifully written *Letters from an American Farmer* was published in 1782; some of the book was written before the onset of the revolutionary war in 1775, some afterward.

When the immigrant lands in America, wrote Crevecoeur, he beholds a garden place, only recently transformed from a wilderness thanks to the honest toil of the inhabitants. Stretched before him are "fair cities, substantial villages, extensive fields, an immense country filled with decent houses, good roads, orchards, meadows, and bridges where a hundred years ago all was wild, woody, and uncultivated." America, he said, is a country of free and independent farmers. Some few townsfolk aside,

We are all tillers of the earth, from Nova Scotia to West Florida. We are a people of cultivators, scattered over an

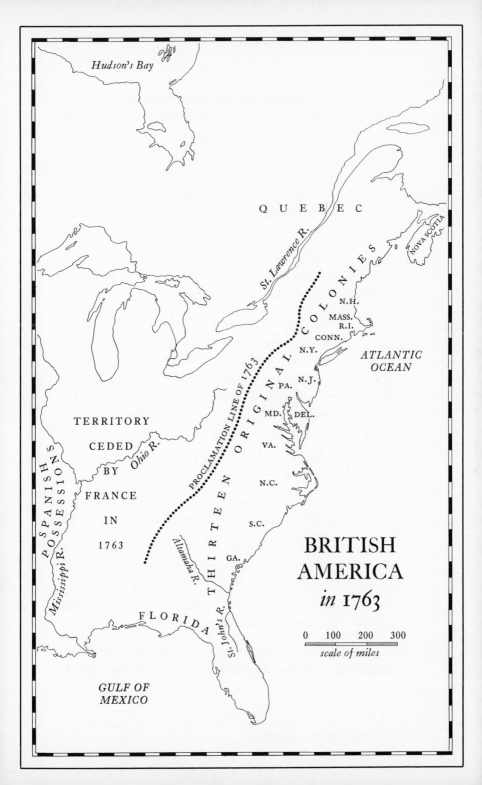

Hudson's Bay

QUEBEC

NOVA SCOTIA

St. Lawrence R.

O R I G I N A L   C O L O N I E S

N.H.
MASS.
R.I.
CONN.
N.Y.

ATLANTIC
OCEAN

PROCLAMATION LINE OF 1763

PA.
N.J.
MD. DEL.

TERRITORY

CEDED

BY

FRANCE

IN

1763

Ohio R.

VA.

N.C.

S.C.

GA.

T H I R T E E N

Altamaha R.

St. John's R.

SPANISH'S
POSSESSIONS

Mississippi R.

FLORIDA

GULF OF
MEXICO

BRITISH
AMERICA
in 1763

0   100   200   300
scale of miles

immense territory, communicating with each other by means of good roads and navigable rivers, united by the silken bands of mild government, all respecting the laws, without dreading their power, because they are equitable. We are all animated with the spirit of an industry which is unfettered and unrestrained, because each person works for himself.

Crevecoeur stressed, almost with elation, that in the world of British America a man did not toil, as the French peasants did, merely that kings, priests, and landlords might live in idleness and wealth:

The rewards of [a man's] industry follow with equal steps on the progress of his labor; his labor is founded on the basis of nature, self-interest; can it want a stronger allurement? Wives and children, who before in vain demanded of him a morsel of bread, now fat and frolicsome, gladly help their father to clear those fields whence exuberant crops are to arise to feed and clothe them all, without any part being claimed either by a despotic prince, a rich abbot, or a mighty lord.

And he noted, in the midst of all this ceaseless toil, a fascinating variety and diversity in American rural life:

Here they live by fishing on the most plentiful coasts in the world; there they fell trees, by the sides of large rivers, for masts and lumber; here others convert innumerable logs into the best boards; there again others cultivate the land, rear cattle, and clear large fields.

Crevecoeur idealized the simple equality of the American farmer, but this does not mean that he was unaware of sharp differences and even bitter conflicts among the colonial people. Frontiersmen and pioneers, for example, he thought of as a different and lower class, "the most vicious of our people." Let the immigrant, he said, proceed inland, and he will come, in the course of time, to the last inhabited districts and to the frontier. These wild woods, he thought, were the final refuge of shiftless, dissolute, idle, and criminal men. They lived rude lives, in part clearing the forest and planting crops, in part with gun in hand, hunting wild animals and game. They despoiled the Indians of their land, sometimes by fraud and if necessary by force. Their hand was against every man's and every man's was against them.

We do not know exactly how many of the American people were living under frontier conditions at the time of the Revolution, but doubtless the number was large. These pioneers were the poorest and the most downtrodden among the white people. Recent immigrants from Europe, servants and apprentices who had earned their freedom or were fleeing from service, fugitives from law, debtors, ruined persons, and social misfits—all were constantly migrating to the back country. There, far from the affluent towns, the fertile plantations, and the prosperous farms of the lowlands, they eked out a rude and dangerous existence as woodsmen, herdsmen, and cultivators.

The life of such people has been painted for us, vividly and with angry compassion, in the journal and other writings of Charles Woodmason, who left the luxuries of Charleston, South Carolina, to work as a missionary for six years (1766–1772) among the settlers in the wild woods of the South Carolina Piedmont—on the Broad and Saluda rivers, along the upper Salkehatchie and the Pee Dee, in District Ninety-Six and the Waxhaws, along the Congaree.

On September 16, 1766, Woodmason, about forty-six years of age, arrived at Pinetree Hill, the center of his district. His aim was to preach to the settlers, encourage agriculture, see to the building of meetinghouses, unite men and women in the sacrament of marriage, baptize infants, visit the sick, and provide a Christian burial for the dead. Woodmason found that the country had been both rapidly and recently settled: "Not many years past," he wrote in his journal, "[this country] was a desert and forest, overrun with wild beasts, and men more savage than they, but now peopled and planted to a degree incredible for the short space of time." All—Welsh, Irish, German, French, and American settlers—lived in extreme poverty, crowded into their roughly constructed cabins and huts. They raised what crops they could, grazed cattle and hogs, exported lumber.

There were, of course, in such new and primitive settlements on the South Carolina frontier absolutely no community facilities: no schools, no courts of law, no meetinghouses or other public buildings except an occasional tavern, no hospitals, and no roads except the rough forest trails. There might be bridges across the rivers and streams, but like as not these would be swept out during the torrential floods of winter and spring. "I was obliged," wrote Woodmason in February 1767, "to swim both self and horses over Lynch's Creek and Black Creek—the swamps full of water, bridges carried away, and riding for miles to the skirts in mud and water." Not infrequently the pastor lost his way in the thicket: "For want of guides," he said, on that same February day in 1767, "and not knowing the country or understanding their directions, I lost myself in the woods, for here are no roads, only small paths, in many places grown up with grass or cover'd with leaves and undiscernible. I got to a cabin at night, and sat up by the fire."

Woodmason was well received by the people in many places (though by no means all). He recorded that large throngs would gather to hear his sermons and that wherever he went he would be pressed to speak. "Many of these people," he recorded, "walk ten or twelve miles with their children in the burning sun—ought such to be without the word of God, when so earnest, so desirous of hearing it and becoming good Christians and good subjects?" But the poverty and rude manners of the settlers sorely tried him. He lamented on one visit:

They are the lowest pack of wretches my eyes ever saw, or that I have ever met with in these woods, as wild as the very deer. [There is] no making of them to sit still during service, but they will be in and out, forward and backward the whole time (women especially) as bees to and fro in their hives. . . . How would the polite people of London stare, to see the females (many very pretty) come to service in their shifts and a short petticoat only, barefooted and barelegged, without caps or handkerchiefs, dressed only in their hair, quite in a state of nature, for nakedness is counted as nothing, as they sleep all together in common in one room, and shift and dress openly with-

out ceremony. The men appear in frocks or shorts and long trousers, no shoes or stockings.

In the winters these people inevitably suffered severely, with little or no bedding, drafty cabins, half-naked children. When people became sick, the remedy was simple. "There you must lie," Woodmason wrote, "til Nature gets the better of the disease, or death relieves you." Though some of the settlers enjoyed abundant fare—milk, butter, eggs, cornmeal, and pork—Woodmason took his own eating utensils with him on his trips. "In many places," he said, "they have nothing but a gourd to drink out of, not a plate, knife, or spoon, a glass, cup, or anything."

Frontier communities were beset with fear and insecurity. Outlaws, criminals, and thieves organized themselves into gangs to prey upon the settlers, and this aroused Woodmason's fury. "On every one of these rivers," he cried,

What numbers of idle, profligate, audacious vagabonds! Lewd, impudent, abandon'd prostitutes, gamblers, gamesters of all sorts—horse thieves, cattle stealers, hog stealers . . . All in a manner useless to society, but very pernicious in propagating vice, beggary, and theft: still more pernicious as we have frequently found, when united in gangs and combinations . . . broke every prison almost in America, whipped in every province, and now set down here as birds of prey to live on the industrious and the painstaking.

The frontier, then, was a community that needed not only religion and education but law and security for life and property—it needed *regulation*. When the people's urgent pleas for help from the provincial government in Charleston went unanswered, they organized a movement of protest and called themselves Regulators; Charles Woodmason was one of their spokesmen.

Woodmason was angered at the total indifference of the Charleston gentry to the sufferings of the white people in the back country; Crevecoeur attacked them for their treatment of the slaves. As already noted, there were half a million black slaves in British America in 1763. They were employed as workers in every one of the mainland colonies—even New England's tiny coastal islands, such as Block Island, had their quota of black men and women to build stone walls and care for horses and cattle. Nonetheless, the majority of the slaves were used on the rice, tobacco, and indigo plantations of the South. Charleston, South Carolina, America's fourth city in size, with a population of 8,000 in 1763, was a prime cultural center for the plantation aristocrats who rose to fame and fortune thanks to the toil of black Americans. "The inhabitants," wrote Crevecoeur, "are the gayest in America; it is called the centre of our beau monde, and it is always filled with the richest planters of the province, who resort hither in quest of health and pleasure."

But, he reflected bitterly, this gaiety and luxury of the Southern planter had for its foundation the toil, penury, and suffering of the slave.

While all is joy, festivity, and happiness in Charleston, would you imagine the scenes of misery overspread in the

A young Maryland aristocrat,
Henry Darnall III, with his black slave.
About 1715.

country? *Their ears are by habit become deaf, their hearts are hardened; they neither see, hear nor feel for the woes of their poor slaves, from whose painful labors all their wealth proceeds . . . no one thinks with compassion of those showers of sweat and of tears which from the bodies of Africans daily drop, and moisten the ground they till. . . . The cracks of the whip urging these miserable beings to excessive labor, are far too distant from the gay capital to be heard. . . . They [the slaves] have no time, like us, tenderly to rear their helpless offspring, to nurse them on their knees, to enjoy the delight of being parents. Their paternal fondness is embittered by considering that if their children live, they must live to be slaves like themselves; no time is allowed to them to exercise their pious office, the mothers must fasten them on their backs, and with this double load follow their husbands into the fields.*

The American slave, said Crevecoeur, was a beast of burden. But in his own African land he had been innocent and free. Captured by force and fraud, he was torn from his family, branded like cattle, taken across the sea, and sold to white men who had no other power over him than that of violence. "If I were possessed of a plantation," he concluded, "and my slaves treated in general as they are here, never could I rest in peace; my sleep would be perpetually disturbed by a retrospect of the frauds committed in Africa in order to entrap them, frauds surpassing in enormity everything which a common mind can possibly conceive."

Crevecoeur not only visited and observed the ways of landsmen who rarely, if ever, saw the sea, but he has left us his impressions of American seamen who rarely saw anything else. He visited Nantucket, an island shaped like a harpoon's head that lies out in the Atlantic fifteen miles south of Cape Cod, and recorded the lives of the Nantucketers with admiration mingled with awe.

The Nantucketers were already well known, even in the revolutionary days, as the world's most daring whaler-men. But they had acquired their skill in hunting whales only slowly, at the cost of long effort and painful experience. Nantucket was occupied in the seventeenth century, like other New England villages and islands, by "proprietors" who divided the land into lots for settlement and use. But Nantucket was a mere sandspit in the ocean; its inhabitants could not look for a livelihood to farming or the pasturing of cattle, but only to the sea. "The first proprietors of this island," wrote Crevecoeur,

began their career of industry with a single whale boat, with which they went to fish for cod; the small distance from their shores at which they caught them, enabled [the Nantucketers] soon to increase their business, and those early successes first led them to conceive that they might likewise catch the whales, which hitherto sported undisturbed on their banks. After many trials . . . they succeeded; thus they proceeded step by step; the profits of one successful enterprise helped them purchase and prepare better materials for a more extensive one . . . By degrees they went a-whaling to Newfoundland, to the Gulf of St. Lawrence, to the Straits of Belle Isle, to the coast of Labrador, to Davis's Straits, even to Cape Desolation, in 70° of latitude, where the Danes carry on some fisheries in spite of the perpetual severities of the inhospitable climate. *In process of time they visited the western islands, the latitude of 34° famous for [the whale], the Brazils, the coast of Guinea.*

Thus by the time of the Revolution, Nantucketers had made the entire Atlantic from the frozen shores of the north to Cape Horn in the south their hunting ground. Whaling, of course, was a dangerous business, but also a very profitable one—in those days when there was no electricity people had to light their houses with candles or oil lamps; whale oil was highly valued because it burned with a bright, pure, odorless flame. Successful Nantucket merchants and sea captains lived in quiet prosperity on their island home; their children were bred to the sea, and followed in their footsteps. "These children," wrote Crevecoeur,

born by the sea-side, hear the roaring of its waves as soon as they are able to listen; it is the first noise with which they become acquainted. . . . They often hear their fathers recount the adventures of their youth, their combats with the whales; and these recitals imprint on their opening minds an early curiosity and taste for the same life. They often cross the sea to go to the mainland, and learn even in those short voyages how to qualify themselves for longer and more dangerous ones.

Thousands of men in colonial America earned their living by sailing before the mast. They went to sea for a variety of reasons; some men fled to it for the same reasons that others fled to the frontier—they were jailbreakers, fugitives from justice, escaped servants. Some such people worked for Nantucketers; Indians and black men, who stood at the bottom of the American social scale, were accounted their best and most skilled harpooneers. But seamanship in Nantucket was also a family tradition. "The motives," noted Crevecoeur, "that lead them to the sea are very different from those of most other seafaring men. It is neither idleness nor profligacy that sends them to that element [but] a settled plan of life, a well-founded hope of earning a livelihood. They go to whaling with as much pleasure, with as strong an expectation of success, as a landsman undertakes to clear a piece of swamp."

Observations of men like Crevecoeur and Woodmason reveal to us that British America in 1763 was an underdeveloped country whose people, of European and African origin, followed a uniquely American existence but had developed marked differences in social status and were enmeshed in their own divisions and hostilities. Yet Crevecoeur thought of Americans, at this early time in our history, as a single people, united by common experiences, common needs, the common compulsions of a new land; bound together, too, by their common tongue, common law, common culture, and common religion that the whites had brought from Europe and that in time were adopted by the blacks or imposed upon them.

How these people, in spite of their own internal differences, their own economic, demographic, and military weaknesses, made a successful revolution against the world's mightiest and wealthiest power is the story of this book.

UNLICENSED LIBERTY
The New Imperial Policy, 1763–1765

*Methinks I see in my mind a noble and puissant nation
rousing herself like a strong man after sleep, and shaking
her invincible locks.*

John Milton, "*Areopagitica*: A Speech for the
Liberty of Unlicensed Printing, to the
Parliament of England," London, 1644

In 1763 the bloody war that had been fought for more
than seven years between Great Britain and France came
to an end. By the Treaty of Paris, France abandoned
all her possessions in North America. Henceforth the
white flag with golden lilies would no longer float over
Canada and the huge inland empire lying between the
Great Lakes and the Gulf of Mexico. All of North
America east of the Mississippi now became the property
of Britain.

Britain and her American colonists had fought side by
side to conquer the French. But from the common victory flowed a fatal division that led directly to the Revolution. To whom did these conquered lands of the
Mississippi Valley rightfully belong? Who should enjoy

them? What should be done with them?

To most Americans in 1763 such questions would have seemed silly. To them it was obvious that the lands won from the French ought to be cleared and settled by the colonists. American land speculators had been dreaming for years about buying up huge tracts of land beyond the Appalachians and selling them off to the settlers who would pour in. Now, in 1763, the opportunity had come.

In Britain there were influential people who looked at all this with different eyes. British fur traders were organized into a powerful lobby, the Hudson's Bay Company, which exercised continuous but secret power over the imperial government. These people opposed the colonization of the virgin lands won from France. The reason for their opposition was obvious enough. When settlers came into forest lands they brought axes. They drove out the Indians, they chopped down the trees, and they killed the squirrels and other furry animals. But trees, Indians, and furry animals formed the natural habitat upon which traders relied for a continuing supply of furs. The furry animals lived among the trees, the Indians caught the furry animals, the traders bought the furs from the Indians and exported them to Europe.

Fur traders, therefore, wished to bar any further American advance across the Appalachians. But other people in England, mainly manufacturers, did not agree with this position. They believed that the westward movement of the Americans should be encouraged—to some extent. The development of farming communities, they reasoned, would mean a rapidly growing colonial population and, therefore, an expanding market for English-made axes, clothing, blankets, clocks, glassware, horseshoes, and tea kettles. And wasn't that what the British Empire was for—to help manufacturers sell their stuff to colonials at a decent profit?

Although there was some disagreement between the fur people and the manufacturers about the future of the American west, they all agreed on one thing, and this is the important point: the new empire must be developed under constant and careful supervision from London. There must be no wild cutting-down of forests; no Yankee manufactures must be allowed to grow up and challenge the British monopoly of the expanding American market.

The insistence of the British authorities upon ruling the colonies with a firm hand, so that the colonists' needs and interests would continue to be subordinated to British ones, was known as "the new imperial policy." American opposition to this policy sparked a resistance movement that led finally to the Revolution.

One of the most dramatic of the new measures was the royal proclamation of October 1763, in which King George III forbade Americans to move across the mountains into the Mississippi Valley until further notice: "Whereas," said the king,

it is just and reasonable, and essential to our interest, and the security of our colonies, that the several nations and tribes of Indians with whom we are connected, and who live under our protection, should not be molested or disturbed in the possession of such parts of our dominions as . . . are reserved to them, or any of them, as their *hunting grounds; we do therefore, with the advice of our Privy Council, declare it to be our royal will and pleasure, that no governor or commander-in-chief . . . in any of our colonies or plantations in America, do presume for the present, and until our further pleasure be known, to grant warrants of survey, or pass patents for any lands beyond the heads of sources of any of the rivers which fall into the Atlantic Ocean from the west and north-west . . .*

All these lands west of the Appalachians, said the king, were for the present to remain under royal control, and reserved for the use of the Indians:

And we do hereby strictly forbid, on pain of our displeasure, all our loving subjects from making any purchases or settlements whatever, taking possession of the lands above reserved, without our especial leave and license for that purpose first obtained. And we do further strictly enjoin and require all persons whatever, who have either willfully or inadvertently seated themselves upon any lands within the countries above described . . . forthwith to remove themselves from such settlements.

A second step in the new imperial policy, taken at the same time, was to expand the British military establishment in America to 10,000 men, stationed principally along the seaboard. This army, the government said, was necessary for defense against the French and the Indians; but it is doubtful if this explanation really fooled anybody. The French, after all, had just left, sailed off to

Europe across the green Atlantic seas. As for the Indians, they certainly presented a real danger to settlers; but most of them were out west, beyond the Appalachians, where very few British troops were stationed. In any event, it was the colonists themselves, through their own militia organization, who had over the years provided the main defense against Indian attack. They had no particular need of British help at this late date.

But there was another reason for the British to set up a peace-time army, and Americans raised the question instantly: Could it be that such an army was designed for use against the colonists themselves?

The British administration in London was asking itself a different question at the end of 1763: Who was to pay for this new standing army? The English taxpayer, usually a landowner, was already heavily burdened, and he would not submit to further taxes without making a tremendous fuss. The easiest and most logical thing to do, as George Grenville saw it—he was Chancellor of the Exchequer and First Lord of the Treasury—was to make the Americans themselves pay for the protection that the empire saw fit to bestow upon them. Hence the third step in the new imperial policy was a series of measures to provide money for the upkeep of the troops. The most important of these was the Stamp Act, which was passed in March 1765 after months of debate and discussion.

The Stamp Act contained fifty-four provisions for the payment of taxes on the use of paper or parchment in the daily business and amusements of the American people. A man must pay a tax on each newspaper or pamphlet he bought; he must pay a tax on every title to land, and on many other legal transactions; he must pay a tax on liquor licenses, on playing cards, calendars, and even dice.

> Be it enacted, by the King's most excellent Majesty, by and with the advice and consent of the lords spiritual and temporal, and commons, in this present Parliament assembled, and by authority of the same, that from the first day of November, one thousand seven hundred and sixty-five, there shall be raised, levied and collected, and paid unto his Majesty, his heirs and successors, throughout the colonies and plantations in America . . .
>
> [14] For every skin, or piece of vellum or parchment, or sheet or piece of paper, on which shall be engrossed, written, or printed any note or bill of lading, which shall be signed for any kind of goods, wares or merchandise, to be exported from, or any cocket or clearance granted within the said colonies and plantations, a stamp duty of four pence.
>
> [18] For every skin, or piece of vellum or parchment, or sheet or piece of paper, on which shall be engrossed, written, or printed any license for retailing spirituous liquors, to be granted to a person who shall take out the same, within the said colonies and plantation, a stamp duty of twenty shillings.
>
> [29] For every skin, or piece of vellum or parchment, or sheet or piece of paper, on which shall be engrossed, written, or printed any original grant or any deed, mesne [land] conveyance, or other instrument whatsoever, by which any quantity of land not exceeding

*A superb oaken carving of a British Lion,
that decorated the stern of an
eighteenth-century sailing vessel.*

100 acres shall be granted, conveyed, or assigned
. . . a stamp duty of one shilling and six pence.

[42] For and upon every pack of playing cards, and all
dice, which shall be sold or used within the said
colonies and plantations, the several stamp duties
following:

[43] For every pack of cards, one shilling.

[44] For every pair of such dice, ten shillings.

[45] And for and upon every paper called a pamphlet,
and upon every news paper containing public news
or occurrences, which shall be printed, dispersed,
and made public, within any of the said colonies
and plantations . . . the respective duties following:

[46] For every such pamphlet and paper, contained in a
half-sheet or lesser piece of paper . . . a stamp duty
of one-half penny for every printed copy.

[47] For every such pamphlet and paper (being larger
than a half-sheet and not exceeding one whole
sheet) . . . a stamp duty of one penny for every
printed copy.

[50] For every almanac or calendar, for any one particular year, or for any time less than a year, which shall
be written or printed on one side only of any one
sheet, skin, or piece of paper, parchment, or vellum,
within the said colonies or plantations, a stamp duty
of two pence.

To make clear the precise purpose for which the funds
thus raised were intended, the act ended with these
words: "The produce of all the aforementioned duties

shall be paid into his Majesty's treasury, and there be held in reserve to be used from time to time by the Parliament for the purpose of defraying the expenses necessary for the defense, protection, and security of the said colonies and plantations."

As to the method of collecting all these taxes, it was simple enough. The stamps were printed in Great Britain on sheets of various values ranging from a halfpenny to two pounds sterling. Stamp collectors were then appointed in each colony to receive the stamps, stock them, and sell them to the people obliged by law to use them. A newspaper editor, for example, would have to affix a one-penny stamp to every copy of his paper that he distributed for sale.

News of the passage of the Stamp Act reached the colonies early in May 1765. There was a good deal of grumbling in the newspaper and pamphlet press; it seemed, for a while, that the Americans would blow off steam but otherwise accept the new law without serious opposition.

In Williamsburg, Virginia, where the House of Burgesses was in session, the early southern spring had come. The land was in full bloom. The little town that had served as the capital since 1698 boasted no more than 300 houses. It was situated between the York and James rivers, in a countryside of lofty trees and spreading tobacco plantations. There was one long street, with the Capitol, where the burgesses sat, at one end and the College of William and Mary at the other. In between, set a little back from the road, was the governor's palace. "All the public edifices," we are told,

are built of brick, but the generality of the houses are of wood, chiefly painted white, and are every one detached from each other; which, with the street deep with sand (not being paved) makes a singular appearance to an European; and is very disagreeable to walk in, especially in summer, when the rays of the sun are intensely hot, and not a little increased by the reflection of the white sand . . . and where there is no shade or shelter to walk under, unless you carry an umbrella.

There, in the spring of 1765, the burgesses were plodding irritably through routine business, anxious to finish the session and leave town before the weather became excessively warm. On May 9 they listened to a petition from John Patrick, "praying to be paid for a horse impressed into the service of the colony in the year 1761, and appraised at 12 pounds." The following day came a complaint from Simon Powell, "setting forth that he was a sergeant in a company of rangers under the command of Captain Hog, and that by the hard duty, and long marches across the mountains and water courses, is thereby rendered infirm, and not able to subsist by his own means."

The burgesses refused to pay for Patrick's horse or to compensate Powell for his rheumatism; but there were other claims that had to be considered more carefully. On May 18, for example, they listened to the plea of Thomas Brown, stating "that he was a soldier under Col. George Washington, and received many wounds in the service, which has occasioned the loss of the use of some of his limbs." And on May 22, the widow Ashby sought payment because her husband Nimrod, a militia commander, "was attacked by a party of Indians who murdered him and took from him all his money to the amount of 66 or 67 pounds."

Other matters had to be taken up that were not con-nected with the recent wars. On May 25 the pilots who made their living guiding ocean-going vessels through Chesapeake Bay petitioned for an increase of pay for the hard and dangerous work of winter pilotage. "The masters of vessels," said the pilots,

are backward in taking a pilot down the bay in summer season, but very fond of it in winter, where we must be obliged to attend them with our boats, and have no harbor to make, let the weather be never so severe, when we part with the ship, for which reason we would sooner carry a ship down the bay for £5 in the summer season, than for £10 in the winter . . . We beg that you will consider the hardships that we must undergo in going down the bay in winter season, for so small a trifle as we get for it, especially in stormy weather, when those that are in their houses think themselves in danger; and what must we think of it in our little decked boats in such a bleak place . . .

The final week of the legislative session began on Monday, May 27. Some of the burgesses had already packed up and left town. One young freshman recently elected from Louisa County had just arrived—lawyer Henry. Angered by the absence of open political opposition to the Stamp Act, Patrick Henry determined to take a stand. On Wednesday, May 29, he submitted to the House five resolutions stating bluntly that

the General Assembly of this colony have the only and sole exclusive right and power to lay taxes and impositions upon the inhabitants of this colony, and that every attempt to vest such power in any person or persons whatsoever, other than the General Assembly aforesaid, has a manifest tendency to destroy British as well as American freedom.

Henry's action touched off a violent debate of which there is no exact record, but the memories of which still echo in history. "Tarquin and Julius Caesar," thundered the young orator, "each had his Brutus; Charles I had his Cromwell; and, I doubt not, but some good American will stand up in favor of his country."

Henry's own account of what happened on that day was written down on the back of a copy of the five resolutions found among his papers. This, he wrote, was

the first opposition to the Stamp Act and the scheme of taxing America by the British Parliament. All the colonies, either through fear, or want of opportunity to form an opposition, or from influence of some kind or other, had remained silent. I had been for the first time elected a Burgess a few days before, was young, inexperienced, unacquainted with the forms of the House, and the members that composed it. Finding the men of weight averse to opposition, and the commencement of the tax at hand and that no person was likely to step forth, I determined to venture; and alone, unadvised, and unassisted, on a blank leaf of an old law-book wrote [the resolutions]. Upon offering them to the House violent debates ensued. Many threats were uttered, and much abuse cast on me by the party for submission. After a long and warm contest the resolutions were passed by a small majority, perhaps of one or two only.

These resolutions set the country ablaze. They were picked up and reprinted in newspapers everywhere, some editors embellishing the originals with material far more defiant in tone than anything that the Virginia burgesses had actually passed. The *Newport Mercury*, for example, printed the following: "Resolved, that any person who shall, by speaking or writing, assert or maintain that any person or persons, other than the General Assembly of this Colony, have the power to impose or lay taxation on the people here, shall be deemed an enemy to his Majesty's colony."

In Boston the Massachusetts House of Representatives adopted a "circular letter" drawn up by James Otis. Delegates from all colonies were invited to come together in New York in October to consult about the situation. In Boston, too, the first action committee was set up to carry on agitation against the Stamp Act and to mobilize resistance to its enforcement. Similar groups, which took the name Sons of Liberty, soon organized in many other communities. Thus by midsummer feelings were reaching an ominous pitch, and they were directed mainly against the collectors appointed by the British government to sell the stamps.

The first demonstration against the stamp act was organized by the Sons of Liberty in Boston on August 14, 1765. An effigy of Andrew Oliver, the new collector, was hung up on a large tree—the "Liberty Tree"—on Newbury Street, the main road leading into town. An observer wrote:

This spectacle continued the whole day without the least opposition, though visited by multitudes. About evening a number of reputable people assembled, cut down the said effigy, placed it on a bier, and covering it with a sheet, they proceeded in a regular and solemn manner amidst the acclamations of the populace through the town till they arrived at the Court House, which, after a short pause, they passed, and proceeding down King Street, soon reached a certain edifice then building for the reception of the stamps, which they quickly levelled to the ground it stood on, and with the wooden remains thereof, marched to Fort Hill [where Oliver's house was]. Kindling a noble fire therewith, they made a burnt offering of the effigy.

Twelve days later, on August 26, a band of sailors, servants, mechanics, and apprentices joyfully demolished the home of Lieutenant-Governor Thomas Hutchinson, who had become a target of popular anger because he championed the royal policies. The resisters

broke all the windows, wainscot, partitions, etc., cut down the cupola, and uncovered a great part of the roof, leaving the house a mere shell from top to bottom; broke and destroyed all the furniture, destroyed or carried off all the wearing apparel, jewels, books and papers of every kind belonging to himself and family, drank, took away, or destroyed 8 pipes and 3 quarter casks of wine, and every bottle of liquor, and all provisions and stores of every kind from his cellars; also carried off £900 in money, and all his plate, pillaging and destroying everything in the house.

The people had taken to the streets to protest the government's denial of their rights as true-born Englishmen. But they remained deeply loyal to the Crown—in the English tradition when people have had no vote, and felt that they counted for nothing in the affairs of state, riot and demonstration has been a time-honored way of petitioning for redress. The Prince of Wales's birthday, falling on August 19, right between the two demonstrations of August 14 and 26, was celebrated throughout Boston with great enthusiasm.

In the evening, the young people had a fire in King Street, and while every apartment in town rang with the pious and loyal ejaculations, "God bless our true British King," "Long live their Majesties," "Heaven preserve the Prince of Wales, and all the Royal Family," etc., the same were thundered through every street in the city. High and low, young and old, white and black, bond and free, joined the chorus. The little children who could not speak, laughed, clapped their hands, blew their whistles, and rung their coral bells.

Throughout British America, 1765 was a long hot summer. Everywhere, both in the towns and the country districts, the people took to the streets. Dangling effigies, burning houses, popular processions, and bonfires gave point to the demand for the resignation of the stamp collectors.

At Newport, Rhode Island, the demonstrations obliged the new collector, Augustus Johnson, to resign publicly. "As I find," he wrote on August 29, "my being appointed the Stamp Officer of this Colony, has irritated the people of this town against me, though the office was bestowed unasked on me, and unthought of: and being willing, as far as it is in my power, to restore tranquillity to the town, I do engage, upon my honor, that I will not accept of said office, upon any terms, unless I have your consent for the same."

In New London, Connecticut, the effigy of the collector "was suspended in the air, on a gibbet . . . and after being exposed about an hour, was taken down, and carried through the town, attended by the principal part of its inhabitants." Later the effigy was burned amid the huzzas of the people, who, we are told, "observed the most perfect decorum in all their behavior."

So it was everywhere. At Philadelphia the collector, John Hughes, was driven out of town; at Williamsburg, Colonel Mercer was surrounded by a huge throng and obliged to resign.

The arrival of the stamps by ship from England in October, and the approach of the November 1 deadline for the enforcement of the act, only provided fresh occasions for popular demonstration. In New York when the ship with the stamps came in, "all the vessels in the harbor lowered their colors to signify mourning, lamentation and woe." As November 1 drew near, "papers were stuck up all over the town . . . threatening destruction to every person and his property who should apply for, deliver out, receive, or use a stamp, or should delay the exercise of customary business without them." The total destruction of Vauxhall, the luxurious house of Major James of the Royal Artillery, gave point to the warning:

The multitude burst open the doors, proceeded to destroy every individual article the house contained: the beds they cut open, and threw the feathers abroad; broke all the glasses, china, tables, chairs, desks, trunks, chests, and making a large fire at a little distance, threw in everything that would burn; drank or destroyed all the liquor; and left not the least article in the house which they did not entirely destroy. After which they also beat to pieces all the doors, sashes, window frames and partitions in the house, leaving it a mere shell. Also destroyed the summer-houses, and tore up and spoiled the garden.

By November the movement had secured its objectives all over the nation. It was clear that the people totally defied the law and that the government would not be able to carry it into effect without military force. "There is not one of the persons appointed," wrote the *Pennsylvania Gazette* on October 31, "from New Hampshire to Georgia, that will execute the odious office; so that the stamps are now a commodity nobody knows what to do with, and are more abominable to be meddled with, than if they were infected with pestilence."

Thus the colonies stood firm. Courts were open, newspapers circulating, and people going about their ordinary business. Everywhere they had found unity in opposition to Britain. Merchants had signed agreements not to import British goods until the Stamp Act was repealed. And the Stamp Act Congress, meeting in New York in October, had affirmed, for the whole nation, that American assemblies alone could tax Americans.

In February 1766 the British Parliament bowed to the inevitable, and repealed the act. The news reached the colonies in March, but it was no surprise to the resistance movement. On January 15 John Adams, a Boston lawyer and politician, noted in his diary:

Spent the evening with the Sons of Liberty, at their own apartment in Hanover Square, near the Tree of Liberty . . . John Avery, distiller or merchant, of a liberal education, John Smith the brazier, Chase the distiller, Joseph Field master of a vessel, Edes the printer, Henry Bass, George Trott, jeweller, were present. . . . Was very civilly and respectfully treated by all present. We had punch, wine, pipes, and tobacco, biscuit and cheese, etc. . . . They chose a committee to make preparations for grand rejoicings upon the arrival of the news of a repeal of the Stamp Act and I heard afterwards they are to have such illuminations, bonfires, pyramids, obelisks, such grand exhibitions, and such fireworks, as were never before seen in America.

So, in the event, it proved.

☆ *3* ☆

SHAWMUT PENINSULA
The British in Boston, 1767–1770

He has erected a multitude of new offices, and sent hither swarms of officers, to harass our people, and eat out their substance.

He has kept among us, in times of peace, standing armies, without the consent of our legislatures.

Declaration of Independence

After the Stamp Act was repealed in 1766, a new finance minister, Charles Townshend, came into office in England. He suggested a new scheme to tax Americans: Why not, he thought, levy taxes ("duties," as they were called) on goods imported into America from England? An act accordingly was passed by Parliament in June 1767 levying such taxes on glass, tea, paper, and lead. These were luxuries or necessities that the colonists could not produce for themselves, and that they would find it very hard to do without.

The Americans, of course, saw no difference in principle between the Stamp Tax and the Townshend Duties: once more, in 1768, non-importation movements sprang up like mushrooms along the American coast. But this time there was an additional grievance. Townshend set up a special American customs office, with headquarters in Boston, with full powers to stop smuggling and to enforce the collection of all import taxes, old and new. There descended upon America a swarm of British officials enthusiastic to enforce the law and to make themselves rich in the process. There were bribes, fees, and fines to be collected; ships could be seized for technical violations of the law and sold for the benefit of the government and the tax collectors.

In June 1768 a Boston mob demonstrated against the seizure of John Hancock's ship *Liberty* on just such a technicality. The frightened tax collectors—or customs commissioners, as they were called—scuttled off to Castle William in Boston Harbor and sent back word to England that the town was in revolt. The British authorities were not worried by the news: the time had come to teach these revolting colonists a lesson. Boston, which had taken the lead in defiance, would be the first to feel the weight of the royal displeasure.

When the colonists came to Massachusetts Bay in 1630 some of them settled on Shawmut Peninsula and renamed it Boston. Boston in those days was shaped like a great irregular pollywog two miles long, sitting with its tail on the southern shore of the bay and its head thrust northward across the estuary of the Charles River. The town began to grow like any other New England settlement—a long main street with houses on each side, each with its own garden patch or orchard, a meetinghouse, a burial ground, a common for grazing cattle.

But Boston was not destined to remain an ordinary farming village. Set like a bridge athwart the Charles River, it united the scattered settlements on both sides of that stream. The distance by water from Boston to Charlestown, on the northern shore, was only half a mile, and a ferry was soon set up, the proceeds of which went to help maintain John Harvard's college at Cambridge. The town became not only a local thoroughfare, but an international one: the northern half of Shawmut was a gigantic wharf lying in the deep water of the bay. The biggest ocean-going vessels could anchor near it and still enjoy full shelter from the storms and rollers of the Atlantic.

Thus by the time of the Revolution, Boston had become the capital of Massachusetts province and a thriving commercial center that provided a livelihood for a population of 16,000. Many of the vessels that lined its wharves were built in the shipyards of the North End. The stately Town House, at the intersection of Cornhill and King streets, was both a merchant exchange and the headquarters of the provincial government. When the British troops arrived in 1768, admiralty mapmakers busied themselves with the preparation of navigation charts for Boston Harbor. These charts show us the crowded town set amid a cluster of offshore islands and shoals and surrounded, like a mother hen, by tiny villages—Roxbury, Milton, Dorchester, Cambridge, Malden, and Chelsea—nestled among quiet fields, stone walls, and woods.

On September 28, 1768, a British fleet dropped anchor off Castle William, in the outer bay of Boston Harbor. The next day, after the commander had satisfied himself that the water was deep enough, the ships moved up the channel to the edge of Boston itself. "At three o'clock in the afternoon," reported the *Boston Evening Post*,

the Launceston of 40 guns, the Mermaid of 38, Glasgow 20, the Beaver 14, Senegal 14, Bonetta 10, several armed schooners, together with the Romney of 60 guns, and the other ships of war before in the harbor, all commanded by Capt. Smith, came up to town, bringing with them the 14th Regiment (Col. Dalrymple) and the 29th Regiment (Col. Carr); none having been disembarked at Castle Island; so that we now behold Boston surrounded at a time of profound peace, with about 14 ships of war, with springs on their cables, and their broadsides to the town!

On October 1 the troops were landed, some 700 men in all, and marched up to Boston Common "with muskets charged, bayonets fixed, colours flying, drums beating and fifes, etc., playing." One regiment took up temporary quarters in Faneuil Hall, the town market and meetinghouse built by the wealthy merchant Peter Faneuil in 1742, and in the Town House, which served both as a merchant's center and the seat of the provincial government. The other regiment set up its tents on the common. "We now behold," wrote the *New York Journal* on October 20, "the Representatives' Chamber, Court-House and Faneuil Hall, those seats of freedom and justice, occupied with troops, and guards placed at

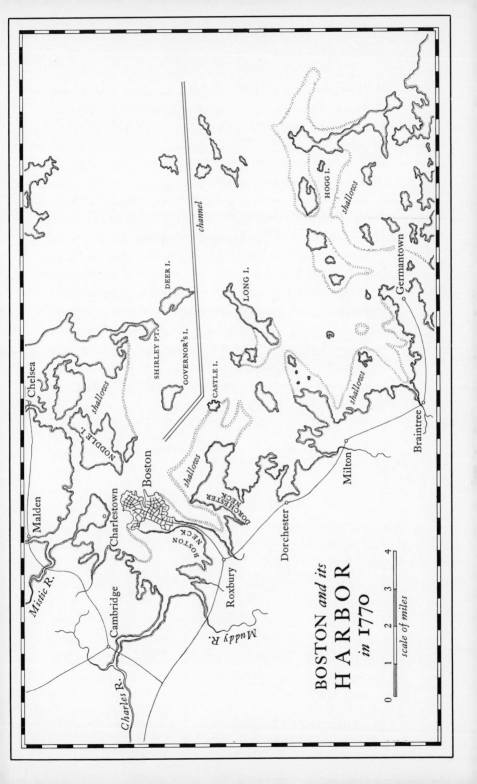

BOSTON *and its*
HARBOR
in 1770

scale of miles

0   1   2   3   4

the doors; the Common covered with tents and alive with soldiers." On November 2 two more regiments, the 64th and 65th, arrived from Ireland with a complement of 1,000 men. Half of these went into barracks on Castle Island, half were quartered in Boston. The town was under military occupation.

The troops remained in Boston for eighteen months; the last of them was not withdrawn until March 1770. In that period the revolutionary sentiments not only of Bostonians but of Americans everywhere became incalculably inflamed.

Boston leaders, with Samuel Adams at their head, planned a campaign of resistance. They prepared the *Journal of Occurrences* to meet the demand throughout the colonies for day-to-day information on the crisis, and published it regularly in the *Boston Evening Post*. The *Journal* was copied by other newspapers and widely read in both America and England. In those days most newspapers appeared only once a week. The *Journal* became a movement organizer: it told people what was being done to resist the British, and how they might help.

The military occupation of Boston showed that the British government was in deadly earnest in its intention to suppress resistance to the customs commissioners and to enforce the collection of duties on imports of manufactured goods from Britain. Here the colonists drew their own conclusions, and they were not the same as the British ones. The British would collect duties on imports? Very well then, the colonists would go without. And that meant that they would either do without the British goods completely, as in the case of glass or paint, or that they would manufacture substitutes of their own.

Hence there developed from 1768 to 1770, under Boston's leadership and example, a fresh movement to boycott British goods and to make in America what had previously been purchased from Britain. This movement concentrated on the manufacture of clothing spun and woven entirely from American wool and linen. The spinning wheel became in 1768 the symbol of the revolutionary movement even as, more than a hundred years later, it became the symbol of India's independence movement under the leadership of Mohandas Gandhi. "Americans," rejoiced the *Journal* in 1769, "are laying a most solid foundation for their future grandeur and felicity, by greatly increasing their growth of hemp and flax, and multiplying their flocks of sheep; spinning schools are opened and filled with learners in Boston and other parts of the province."

The movement for home manufactures was fanned by Sunday sermons, political orations, and college lectures. New England farmers "look upon it as a disgrace if they and their family are not clad with the fleece of their own flock, and by their own industry," wrote the *Journal* in December 1768. This, of course, required much extra work, particularly on the part of the young people. But, to the surprise of many of the teenagers who now flocked to the wheel to learn the art of spinning, it was not as tedious as might have been expected. Girls discovered that the resistance movement was serious business, but also fun. "I found," wrote our anonymous author of the *Journal*, "that as these Daughters of Liberty delight in each other's company, they had agreed to

The tombstone of Ruth Ladd—
Concord, Massachusetts, 1766—portraying a
young girl garlanded with ribbons.

make circular visits to each of their houses, and in order to excite emulation in serving their country . . . had determined to convert each visit into a spinning match."

The spinning matches would start at six in the morning and continue all day. Many skeins of flax and wool would be spun amid the laughter, chatter, and song. In good weather the matches were made delightful by being held outdoors. At Dorchester, we are told, one summer day in 1769 sixty girls

assembled at the house of Rev. Mr. Jonathan Bowman, with wheels, and the greater part of them with flax, and spent the day there in the much-to-be-recommended-and-encouraged business of spinning. The order in which they were ranged on the green, before the house at which they met; the decent behaviour, pleasantry, and industry visible among them in the work of the day, gave sincere and singular pleasure to the numerous surrounding spectators of this and other towns. About sunset the wheels ceased doing. . . . Provision for the repast and entertainment of the ladies was freely sent in and gratefully acknowledged.

In most cases it was girls and young women who took part in this work. At Braintree, we learn, "a young miss of 9 years old wound off her two double skeins, excellently well spun." Many of the seventy-seven girls who joined a spinning bee in the village of Chebacco in July 1769 were no more than thirteen years of age. But older people also took part. From Newport, Rhode Island, came the story of a champion spinner who was between seventy and eighty years of age and who had never spun a thread in her life before. "Thus," exulted the *Journal*, "has the love of liberty and dread of tyranny kindled in the breast of old and young a glorious flame . . ."

The appeal to the people not to buy imported clothing, dresses, and ribbons, as well as other dutiable goods like tea, was also broadcast through a song first published in the *Boston Evening Post* in 1768.

Young Ladies in Town

la - dies in town, and those that live round, Wear none but your own coun-ty lin - en; Of e -

con - o - my boast, let your pride be the most To show

clothes of your own make and spin - ning. What if

home - spun, they say, be not quite so gay As bro-

cades, be not in a pas - sion; For

once it is known, 'tis much worn in town, One and all will cry out, 'tis the fash-ion!

And as one all agree that you'll not married be
    To such as will wear London factory;
But at first sight refuse, tell 'em you will choose
    As encourage our own manufactory.
No more ribbons wear, nor in rich silks appear,
    Love your country much better than fine things;
Begin without passion, 'twill soon be the fashion
    To grace your smooth locks with a twine string.

Throw away your bohea, and your green hyson tea,
    And all things of a new-fashioned duty;
Get in a good store of the choice Labrador
    There'll soon be enough here to suit ye.
These do without fear, and to all you'll appear
    Fair, charming, true, lovely, and clever;
Though the times remain darkish, young men will be sparkish,
    And love you much stronger than ever.

Over the months the *Journal* built up a picture of British tyranny in Boston, thus warning the other colonies of the treatment that they might expect in the absence of united resistance to imperial policies. Bitter complaints were voiced first of all at the high-handed and arbitrary procedures followed by the customs commissioners under the protection of British bayonets. Swarms of revenue officials, it was said, had descended on the helpless town: "The names of the newly-created officers, and the business said to be allotted to them, would make a small revenue dictionary." Boston merchants and their trade were being subjected to a continuous petty, malicious, and crippling harassment. Ships were seized, detained on trifling pretenses, and the owners subjected to fines or confiscation at the discretion of the new admiralty courts. Lamented the *Journal:*

The present trade of America has of late years, been embarrassed beyond description, with the multiplicity and intricacy of regulations and ordinances; [the government] seem to be possessed with something hardly short of a rage, for regulation and restriction. They have . . . multiplied bonds, certificates, affidavits, warrants, sufferances, cockets, etc., and every species of custom-house officers, both upon the land and water; have supported the new regulations with such severe penalties . . . that American commerce is expiring under them.

The *Journal* proceeded, next, to report the existence of friction between the soldiery and the Bostonians, and to voice bitter complaints at the licentious and irreligious behavior of the troops, which disturbed the sober quiet of the Sabbath. Observance of the Sabbath was taken seriously in Puritan Boston, and there were many meetinghouses where divine service was conducted—Old North, Old South, Brattle Street, New North, New South, Hollis Street, Lynde Street meetinghouses. The mood necessary for worship was constantly interrupted by the sacrilegious music of the fife and drum. "This being the Lord's day," recorded the *Journal* on November 6, 1768,

the minds of serious people at public worship were greatly disturbed with drums beating and fifes playing, unheard of before in this land. What an unhappy influence must this have upon the minds of children and others, in eradicating the sentiments of morality and religion, which a due regard to that day has a natural tendency to cultivate and keep alive!

Complaints to the military produced some temporary improvement in the situation, but not for long. In May 1769 the *Journal* had cause to complain once more that the disturbance of public worship continued and that "a party of soldiers with those noisy instruments passed by one of those assemblies [for divine worship] twice in the space of half an hour."

Disturbance of public worship by itself might not have been so very bad. Alas, worse was to come. The soldiers were a debauched, dissolute, and godless crew. They contaminated youth and the lower classes generally not only by their music but by their very presence and example. They strolled around town on Sunday, chewing tobacco (no doubt) and talking in loud voices; they raced horses on the common; and they were perpetually drunk. That the licentiousness of the men was "daily increasing," the *Journal* complained, was due in part to the fact that the army paid no attention to the moral welfare of its troops. "The common soldiers," lamented our author, "are in general destitute of Bibles and proper books of devotion." He suggested that the Society for Propagating the Gospel might devote part of its funds to providing Bibles for the men. They were far too poor, and their pay too meager, to buy such necessities for themselves.

If the army's treatment of its men was clearly un-Christian, it was also cruel and tyrannical. In 1768 and 1769, and throughout the war that was to follow, the British army in America was plagued with a high desertion rate. Its soldiers were drawn from the same class as so many of the colonial immigrants themselves—they were the poorest of the poor, landless peasants from Scotland and Ireland, the sweepings of Britain's lanes and streets "pressed" into service either by false promises or forcible kidnapping at the hands of the recruiting parties. The New World looked as attractive to them as to other immigrants. As winter set in in 1768 and the bay froze in the shallow waters, escape from Boston became an easy matter. "The ice," wrote the *Journal*, "having opened new passages out of town for the soldiery, desertions are more numerous than ever notwithstanding all the care of the officers, and vigilance of the military guards, which almost surround the town."

At Boston, even in peace, the penalty for desertion from the British army was death. This fate befell Private Richard Arnes of the 14th Regiment on October 31, 1768. The entire military garrison marched onto Boston Common in the cold dawn to the roll of drums sounding the dead march. At eight o'clock Private Arnes, dressed in white, was shot by a firing squad. The troops "marched round the corpse as it lay on the ground, when it was put into the coffin which was carried by its sides into the Common, and buried in a grave near where he was shot, and the Church service read over him. This was the first execution of the kind ever seen in this town."

In the eyes of Bostonians the death of this private was close to murder by the Crown. Some of the leading ladies of the town had gotten up a petition to Brigadier-General Pomeroy, commanding, that the man be pardoned—was this not a first offense, and was the country not at peace? "But the numerous desertions from so important a service as the troops are now engaged in" noted the *Journal* with bitter irony, "it seems prevented this act of grace."

Such executions were infrequent in Boston, if only because it was difficult, if not impossible, to find and recapture deserters, and because the country folk showed an understandable reluctance to inform against them. Flogging was a far more usual punishment to enforce discipline and prompt obedience among the men, even for minor offenses. Boston was now treated to the revolting spectacle of men being strung up to the halberts and lashed in public. The halbert was a long wooden lance; three lances were bound at the top to make a tripod, and against this the victim was tied. Hundreds of lashes might be laid on in a single punishment to the accompaniment of the agonizing screams and groans of the victim.

The *Journal* recorded on April 11, 1769:

There were very severe whippings the day before yesterday; a grenadier having received about two hundred lashes, in part of a Court Martial's sentence, the doctor, as it is said, advised to his being loosed from the halberts. . . . He was accordingly unloosed, when he fell upon the ground senseless, but upon pouring some water down his throat, he soon came to himself; this encouraged the humane officer, to order his being again tied to the halberts, and that the drummers should proceed in executing the sentence; he accordingly received fifty more lashes, as seemingly insensible of the strokes as would have been a statue of marble.

This type of violence, so coarsely advertised to all America from Boston Common, added fuel to the flame of hatred that ordinary people now came to feel for the British.

The following song, composed by an English soldier in the mid-eighteenth century, illuminates and protests against the unspeakable brutality practiced by the British army in defense of the empire.

The Deserter

fore _ I did know, ___ It's to the King's _
du - ty I was forced for _ to go.

When first I deserted I thought myself free,
When my cruel companions informed against me:
I was quickly followed after and brought back with speed,
With chains I was loaded, heavy irons on me.

Court martial! court martial! they held upon me,
And the sentence they passed was three hundred and three:
May the Lord have mercy on their souls for their sad cruelty,
For now the King's duty lies heavy on me.

(abridged)

Boston's inhabitants were moved by the sufferings of
the troops; but they hated them, too, as a living expression of Britain's illegal purpose in taxing them. The
common people—sailors, apprentices, serving men, sail-
makers, handicraftsmen, and laborers—flung at them

insults like "lobster" or—in reference to the humiliation of flogging—"bloodyback." These were terms as galling to the trooper as "nigger" to a black man or "fuzz" to a policeman. Clashes between townspeople and troops were frequent, and complaints rained in upon the magistrates. Captain Willson of the 59th Regiment, it was alleged, incited Boston slaves to cut their masters' throats and claim freedom, "to the great terror and danger of the peaceable inhabitants of said town." Riots and tumults occasioned by brawls between the soldiers and the town watch were frequent. Women and girls were insulted, attacked, and raped. In June 1769, it was asserted that:

A woman going to the south-market for a fish, stopped at the shop of Mr. Chase, under Liberty Tree, appearing to be faint. They got some water, but on raising her up, she died instantly. A jury of inquest was summoned, and upon examination she appeared to be one Sarah Johnson, of Bridgewater, on whom it appeared by evidence and several marks, that violence had been perpetrated the 24th inst. by soldiers unknown, which probably was the cause of her death.

The soldiers, poorly paid and hard put to it to find extra jobs, stole from shops and mugged people in the streets. When people, especially boys, taunted them they returned the insults in kind, and sometimes added blows for good measure. "All the insults," concluded the *Journal*, "which the inhabitants of this town are daily receiving from the soldiery cannot be [recorded] in this place." Nor did the people have remedies for the wrongs

A British anti-war cartoon printed
in London, October 1775, shows a British
soldier and his family "exposed to the
horrors of war, pestilence, and famine
for a farthing an hour."

they suffered. What use was it to complain to a magistrate? Boston's "wholesome laws" were powerless against armed might. The arrest of the offenders was difficult; sometimes a man was caught and sentenced, but his buddies descended upon the jail and set him free. How many wrongs, asked the *Journal* ominously, would "a loyal and prudent people bear, before they proceed to extremities?"

It was the evening of March 4, 1770, when the pent-up tensions and hatreds of eighteen months of military occupation came to the point of explosion. The streets were lit by a full moon and carpeted with new-fallen snow. A little after eight o'clock a fray broke out at Murray's barracks on Brattle Street between soldiers of the 29th Regiment quartered there and the townspeople. As had happened so many times before, harsh words filled the air and blows were exchanged. *"Are the inhabitants,"* shouted one man, *"to be knocked down in the streets? Are they to be murdered in this manner?"* Officers of the regiment tried to calm him, but he went on, *"We did not send for you. We will not have you here. We'll get rid of you, we'll drive you away."*

The officers worked hard to bring their angry men under control and to get them back into the barracks, but the confusion increased with the mounting fury of the people. Amid cries of *"To the main guard!"* and the pealing of church bells, the crowd surged down Boylston Alley and converged upon the Custom House in King Street. They were sailors, dockworkers, household servants, young apprentices. Some had picked up sticks, stones, shovels, clubs; one man even had a sword.

At the Custom House they found a lone sentry named Montgomery on duty. A little barber's boy, not more than six or seven years old, who had jeered at an officer a little earlier and had then been clubbed (as he said) by this same Montgomery, raised an accusing finger: *"This is the sonofabitch that knocked me down."* And the crowd howled *"Kill him! Knock him down!"*

The terrified Montgomery stumbled up the Custom House steps and drummed on the door with his gun butt. Then he turned, primed and loaded his weapon, and yelled at the top of his lungs, *"Turn out the main guard!"* At the guard post across the street Captain Preston took charge, and marched out the relief, seven men in all, who ranged themselves in an arc on the steps of the Custom House with bayonets fixed and guns at the ready. At this the fury of the crowd increased. They answered with a volley of stones, snowballs, oyster shells, and billets of firewood, *"Fire!"* they cried. *"Fire, you bloodybacks, you lobsters. Fire, damn you, fire! You dare not fire."*

What happened then is described by Andrew, the black slave of Oliver Wendell, a Boston selectman. "The people," as Andrew testified at the soldiers' trial,

seemed to be leaving the soldiers, and turning from them, when there came down a number from Jackson's Corner, huzzaing and crying damn them, they dare not fire, we are not afraid of them. One of these people, a stout man with a long cordwood stick, threw himself in and made a blow at the officer. I saw the officer try to fend off the stroke, whether it struck him or not I do not know. The stout man then turned around, and struck the grenadier's gun at the captain's right hand, and immediately fell in with his club, and knocked his gun away, and struck him over the head; the blow came either on the soldier's cheek or hat. This stout man held the bayonet with his left hand, and twitched it and cried, kill the dogs, knock them over. This was the general cry; the people then crowded in.

Andrew then heard a soldier yell *"Fire!"* and the report of a gun. In all, seven shots were fired; five men were killed and three wounded. Among the dead was Crispus Attucks, the "stout man" who had led the attack. We know little else about him beyond the fact that he was a dockworker and probably an ex-slave.

The next fall (September–October 1770) Captain Preston and the soldiers of the guard were placed on trial on a charge of willful murder. To the dismay of the Bostonians the soldiers were defended by two leaders of the revolutionary cause, lawyers Josiah Quincy and John Adams. Adams was aghast at the confrontation that had occurred between the "mob" and the empire. He wished to prove that not the town but lawless individuals were responsible for the riot. Punishment, he felt, should not be inflicted upon the soldiers; had they not acted only in self-defense, and out of mortal terror for their lives? If they were guilty of anything, he argued, it was "justifiable homicide," which he explained as follows:

Halberts from the French and Indian Wars.

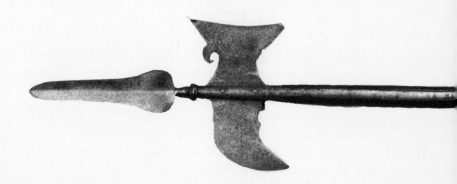

They had a right to kill in their own defense; if [the assault] was not so severe as to endanger their lives, yet if they were assaulted at all, struck and abused by blows of any sort, by snowballs, oyster shells, cinders, clubs or sticks of any kind; this was a provocation, for which the law reduces the offense of killing, down to manslaughter, in consideration of those passions in our nature, which cannot be eradicated.

As for Crispus Attucks, no one spoke for him, but only his death. Like John Brown years later, Attucks showed men the way to die if they would win freedom.

Captain Preston and six of the guard were acquitted; two men (one of whom was Montgomery) were convicted of manslaughter, and received a suspended sentence. Perhaps the most remarkable thing about the whole episode was that the soldiers were placed on trial at all. The British army had been sent to Boston to cow the town with a show of force; and the army was arrested, sent to jail, and indicted on a murder charge. A ridiculous and humiliating conclusion for a military expedition!

☆ *4* ☆

TO LEXINGTON AND BACK
The Tea Party, and What Came of It, 1773–1775

He has abdicated government here, by declaring us out of his protection, and waging war against us.

Declaration of Independence

After the Boston confrontation, quiet settled for a while on the American colonies. The non-importation associations that had been organized earlier to boycott the import and sale of British goods were dissolved. The British government removed the offending duties on paper and glass, retaining only the three-pence-per-pound tax on tea. In this way the Crown made a conciliatory gesture toward the colonists while at the same time affirming its supremacy over British America and its right to impose taxes there at will.

Around the tea tax came the next confrontation, the next test of strength between colonists and Crown. By 1773 the East India Company, which had enjoyed a monopoly of carrying tea from India for sale in England and her dependencies, was in distress. The company found itself with great quantities of tea on its hands that it could not sell at a profit, and it was facing bankruptcy. It petitioned the British government for relief, and was granted the right to export its tea directly to the American colonies without having—as had previously been the case—to pay duties to the authorities in England on the way. What the company was granted was the right to sell unlimited quantities of tea at a very low price on the American market. This tactic, which sometimes has real advantages in the business world, is known as "dumping"; to the British government it seemed that granting permission to dump East India tea on the colonies would benefit all concerned.

In the first place, the East India Company stood to gain new outlets for its tea; the tea could be sold so cheaply that the smuggled Dutch teas that the colonists were then using would be undersold and driven from the market. Second, the British government would collect threepence for each pound of tea entered at the American ports; the calculation was precisely this—that the East India tea could be sold cheaper than Dutch tea *even though it paid the threepence-per-pound import duty*. This would both provide revenue for the king's money box and vindicate his claim that he *did* have the right to tax Americans. And, third, the colonists would have nothing to complain about because, even if they were paying a tax, they would still be getting tea more cheaply than they had ever gotten it before.

The only trouble with this perfect scheme was that it was just a shade too smart, for it spelled the ruin of the American merchants, John Hancock of Boston among them, who were making lots of money smuggling

Dutch tea, and having fun doing it. These people may not have had any formal training in economic theory, but it did not take a business wizard to see that once the American merchants were ruined and the Dutch tea driven out, the East India Company would have a monopoly of the American tea trade and, presto, the price of tea would rise again. To cap it all, the colonists saw here another underhanded scheme to tax British America illegally, and they weren't falling for it.

In October 1773 the East India Company dispatched its tea ships to Charleston, Philadelphia, Boston, and New York. The first sign of resistance came in Philadelphia on October 18. A mass meeting assembled in the State House and called for the resignation of the agents of the East India Company—"consignees," as they were called—who had been appointed to receive and sell the tea on the company's behalf. On the following November 5 the Boston resistance, under the leadership of Samuel Adams, followed Philadelphia's lead; the people, assembled in town meeting in Faneuil Hall, asked the company's Boston consignees to resign. This the consignees, who included Governor Thomas Hutchinson himself, refused to do. Clearly Boston was headed for a confrontation if, when the tea arrived, the people refused to allow it to be landed and the governor refused to let it be returned to England.

On Sunday, November 28, 1773, the tea ship *Dartmouth* put into Boston Harbor laden with 114 chests of tea. The next morning thousands of Bostonians and people from the neighboring towns of Dorchester, Roxbury, Brookline, Cambridge, and Charlestown poured into the Old South Meeting House at the corner of Milk and Marlborough Streets. The meeting resolved that the tea could not be landed, and that it must be sent back. A guard was set over the *Dartmouth*, which lay at Griffin's Wharf, to make sure that none of the cargo was put ashore.

This turn of events did not worry Governor Hutchinson unduly. If the tea was not landed, the ship would not receive clearance (permission to sail) from the harbor authorities; then, under the revenue laws, the cargo would be subject to confiscation by the revenue officers twenty days after arrival, that is, on December 17. The tea could then be given over to the consignees and sold.

Then, early in December, two more tea ships arrived and tied up at Griffin's Wharf. Governor Hutchinson alerted two men o' war, *Active* and *Kingfisher*, to patrol the ship channel and prevent these ships from making a getaway without unloading their cargo. This was a necessary precaution, for the sea captains and ship owners were far from happy at being caught in the middle of a hassle between the governor and the Bostonians. Every day that they had to cool their heels in the harbor was costing them money in crew's wages and lost time; the temptation must have been great to slip away unnoticed if they possibly could.

On December 15 Francis Rotch of Nantucket, who was captain of the *Dartmouth*, was flatly and finally refused permission to clear harbor with the tea aboard. On December 16 thousands of people, once more assembled in the Old South Meeting House, received the news that clearance had been denied. Seizure of the *Dartmouth* by the revenue authorities and the landing of the tea under the protection of the troops appeared imminent.

Within a few hours of midnight a body of men disguised as Indians and armed with hatchets marched to Griffin's Wharf, took possession of the three tea ships, hoisted 340 chests from the holds, and broke open the contents into Boston Bay. Paul Revere—a Boston silversmith who acted as chief liaison officer for the resistance —galloped off to New York and Philadelphia to bring the news. But similar drastic action was not taken in the other ports; there the consignees wisely resigned, and the tea was either shipped back to London or rotted unsold in the revenue-office cellars.

Many songs were written to commemorate this famous episode in which the defiance of one town sparked the resistance of a continent. One of the most popular songs was "The Rich Lady Over the Sea." It tells, in simple but expressive terms, how the colonists viewed themselves after the Boston Tea Party. They were no longer children, to be ordered about as the "mother country," England, chose; they had grown to manhood and would decide for themselves what to eat or drink, what taxes to pay, whom they should listen to and obey.

The Rich Lady Over the Sea

Voice

(Guitar Instrumental)

There was a rich lad - y lived

o - ver the sea, And she was an is - land

queen; _____ Her daugh-ter lived off in the

new ___ coun-try, With an o - cean of wa - ter be-

tween, With an o - cean of wa - ter be - tween. ___

The old lady's pockets were filled with gold,
      Yet never contented was she;
So she ordered her daughter to pay her a tax
      Of thruppence a pound on the tea.
                    CHORUS
            (*Repeat the last line of each verse.*)

"Oh mother, dear mother," the daughter replied,
      "I'll not do the thing that you ask;
I'm willing to pay a fair price on the tea,
      But never the thruppenny tax."
                    CHORUS

"You shall!" cried the mother, and reddened with rage,
      "For you're my own daughter, you see;
And it's only proper that daughter should pay
      Her mother a tax on the tea."
                    CHORUS

She ordered her servant to be called up
    To wrap up a package of tea;
And eager for thruppence a pound, she put in
    Enough for a large family.

CHORUS

She ordered her servant to bring home the tax,
    Declaring her child must obey,
Or, old as she was, and woman most grown,
    She'd half whip her life away.

CHORUS

The tea was conveyed to her daughter's own door,
    All down by the oceanside;
But the bouncing girl poured out every pound
    On the dark and boiling tide.

CHORUS

And then she called out to the island queen,
    "O mother, dear mother," called she,
"Your tea you may have when 'tis steeped enough,
    But never a tax from me."

CHORUS

News of the destruction of the East India Company's property reached England in January 1774. The British government moved swiftly to crush the Boston "rebellion" and to punish the town for its defiance. A number of laws were put through Parliament inflicting severe penalties upon Boston and Massachusetts; these were known as the Coercive Acts. The Boston Port Act of March 1774, to name one of the Coercive Acts, established a blockade of Boston Harbor and suspended the town's trade with the rest of the world. The act in effect announced the ruin of Boston and the starvation of its inhabitants until such time as the tea was paid for and guarantees given for future good behavior. The act stated that

dangerous commotions and insurrections have been fomented in the town of Boston, in the province of Massachusetts Bay, in New England, by divers ill-affected persons, to the utter destruction of the public peace, and good order of the said town; in which commotions and insurrections certain valuable cargoes of teas, being the property of the East India Company . . . were seized and destroyed.

It forbade the carrying on of any seaborne trade until such time as "full satisfaction hath been made by or on behalf of the inhabitants of the said town of Boston to the United Company of Merchants of England trading to the East India [the East India Company] for the damages sustained by the said Company by the destruction of their goods sent to the said town of Boston."

Another of the Coercive Acts, the Quartering Act of April 1774, authorized the British army to seize buildings for the use of troops and to station armed forces wherever it chose among the civilian population. To ensure that Boston was brought into proper submission by both economic blockade and military occupation, General Thomas Gage, commander-in-chief of His Majesty's forces in North America, was appointed governor of Massachusetts in the place of Thomas Hutchinson. Gage sailed from England with four regiments of troops and landed in Boston on May 17, 1774. By August seven regiments were stationed in Boston.

Two days after Gage arrived, news of the Boston Port Act reached Williamsburg, where the Virginia Assembly was in session. Here, on May 19, 1774, a number of Virginia's leaders, including Patrick Henry, Thomas Jefferson, George Mason, and Richard Henry Lee, met together and discussed what they should do about the Boston crisis. As a result of this meeting Jefferson prepared a resolution, which was submitted to the Assembly on May 24 and promptly passed:

This House, being deeply impressed with apprehension of the great dangers to be derived to British America, from the hostile invasion of the city of Boston, in our sister colony of Massachusetts Bay, whose harbor and commerce are on the 1st day of June next to be stopped by an armed force, deem it highly necessary that the said first day of June be set apart by the members of this House as a day of fasting, humiliation, and prayer, devoutly to implore the divine interposition for averting the heavy calamity, which threatens destruction to our civil rights, and the evils of civil war; to give us one heart and one mind firmly to oppose, by all just and proper means, every injury to American rights.

The resolution was made known throughout Virginia. It meant that the Virginia aristocracy stood united with the merchants and artisans of Massachusetts in open defiance of British authority. The following day, May 25, Governor Dunmore angrily dissolved the Virginia Assembly in punishment for such insolence. But the members of the Assembly refused to be silenced. They reconvened in the Raleigh Tavern, close by the Capitol, and voted for the calling together of a Continental Congress in Philadelphia. To prepare for this, the Assembly issued a summons for a special Virginia convention to meet in Williamsburg in August.

The Virginia action gave great impetus to the movement in all the colonies for unity with Massachusetts and for an all-American resistance to British tyranny. Everywhere patriots and revolutionaries, following the Virginia example, began to call together emergency conventions and to elect delegates to the Continental Congress. The Congress, which met in Philadelphia in September 1774, was composed of fifty-four delegates representing every colony except Georgia. After much discussion it voted to renew the non-importation agreements of 1767, and sent a respectful message to the king requesting a redress of grievances, including repeal of the Coercive Acts. To this petition it added a warning, addressed directly to the people of England, that Americans would not submit to tyranny without resistance:

Permit us to be as free as yourselves; and we shall ever esteem a union with you to be our greatest glory and our greatest happiness. But if you are determined that your ministers shall wantonly sport with the rights of mankind; if neither the voice of justice, the dictates of law, the principles of the constitution, or the suggestions of humanity can restrain your hands from shedding human blood in such an impious cause, we must then tell you that we will never submit to be hewers of wood or drawers of water for any ministry or nation in the world.

Not only in America, but also in England, warning

voices were raised, to make clear to the royal government under Lord North that Americans were in earnest, that they would not be bullied, and that a bloody war was imminent. In December, Benjamin Franklin, Pennsylvania's representative in London, made clear to North that withdrawal of British troops from Boston and the repeal of the Coercive Acts were an absolute condition of successful reconciliation. But the British government turned a deaf ear to his advice and to the petition of the Continental Congress. In February 1775 it declared that Massachusetts was in a state of rebellion.

The American pleas for reconciliation were seconded by Edmund Burke, a great Irish statesman, and one of a small group of doves in Parliament—others were William Pitt, Colonel Isaac Barre, and John Wilkes—who courageously and articulately opposed North's policy of repression. On March 22, 1775, in one of an incomparable series of orations on the American question, Burke vindicated the rights of the American people.

This people, he said, is leaping into nationhood: "Your children do not grow faster from infancy to manhood than they spread from families to communities, and from villages to nations." This rapidly growing population, said Burke, *was in itself a main cause of their resistance* and British efforts to check the advance of settlement in the west through "hoarding of the royal wilderness" would be futile. Suppose, Burke asked, that the Crown refused to grant more land for this purpose,

What would be the consequence? The people would occupy without grants. They have already so occupied in

many places. You cannot station garrisons in every part of these deserts. If you drive people from one place, they will carry on their annual tillage, and remove with their flocks and herds to another. . . . Already they have topped the Appalachian mountains. From thence they behold before them an immense plain, one vast, rich, level meadow. Over this they would wander without a possibility of restraint.

The same boundless energy that was driving the Americans westward to settle the continent was also sending them to the ends of the earth as the world's greatest navigators. Consider, said Burke, their whalers:

While we follow them among the tumbling mountains of ice, and behold them penetrating into the deepest frozen recesses of Hudson's Bay and Davis' Straits, we hear that they have pierced the opposite region of polar cold, that they are at the antipodes, and engaged under the frozen serpent of the south . . . Nor is equinoctial heat more discouraging to them than the accumulated winter of both the poles. While some of them draw the line and strike the harpoon on the coast of Africa, others pursue their gigantic game along the coast of Brazil. No sea but what is vexed by their fisheries; no climate that is not witness to their toils.

The Americans, Burke continued, were not, as the British government vainly imagined, cowards and poltroons. They possessed "a fierce spirit of liberty stronger . . . than in any other people on earth." Precisely because they were descended from Englishmen and were well versed in English law and history, the Americans understood liberty, and advocated it, in accordance with English ideas and on English principles. "The Americans," said he, "augur misgovernment at a distance, and snuff the approach of tyranny in every tainted breeze."

The king and Lord North might dismiss Burke's observations as mere rhetoric, but Thomas Gage could not. In the fall of 1774 the people of the American colonies, and of New England in particular, began to prepare for resistance. As English regiments and artillery poured into Boston, New England towns began to store powder and cannon, and the militia began to drill regularly on the village greens.

The militia system in operation throughout the colonies was almost as old as England itself, and it had been brought to America by the earliest settlers from the old country. Under this system each able-bodied man between the ages, roughly, of sixteen and sixty was obliged to serve in the defense of his own town or village against hostile attack. Each man, under penalty of fines for delinquency, was held responsible for the maintenance of his own equipment—rifle or musket, clothing, bullet molds, and so on. Each man was obliged to present himself on muster days for inspection and drill on the village green or common. The average American, in other words, was a part-time, amateur soldier who took up arms reluctantly, and only when emergency made it necessary. As soon as the crisis was over he put down his gun and returned to his farm or trade.

The fall of 1774 was, for New Englanders, just such an emergency. Militia companies held daily or weekly drills, made bullets, and learned the manual of arms. Some, who held themselves ready to march at a minute's notice, were called "minutemen."

As the year 1775 dawned, General Sir Thomas Gage waited nervously behind his Boston fortifications and awaited further reinforcements. He was uneasily and acutely aware of the open preparations for armed resistance that were going on all all around him. On January 30 Lieutenant Frederick Mackenzie of the 23rd Regiment noted in his diary: "The people are evidently making every preparation for resistance. They are taking every means to provide themselves with arms; and are particularly desirous of procuring the locks of firelocks, which are easily conveyed out of town without being discovered by the guards." British soldiers who sought to supplement their meager pay by selling arms to the people received savage punishments. "A soldier of the 4th Regiment," Mackenzie reported on February 4, 1775, "who was tried a few days ago for disposing of arms to the townspeople has been found guilty and sentenced to receive 500 lashes." When the royal troops went on training marches into the country around Boston, their every move was watched and reported by militiamen on duty for that purpose.

Vengeance was also inflicted upon Americans who were caught buying arms. Thomas Ditson, a farmer who was taken buying a firelock from a private in the 47th Regiment on March 8, 1775, was stripped, tarred and feathered, and paraded by the soldiers all the way through Boston in a cart, much to the indignation of the townspeople. The *New York Journal* reported:

Lady Gage, by John Singleton Copley.
Contrast this "rich lady over the sea"
with the poor soldier's wife (page 57).

The soldiers mounted [Ditson] on a one-horse truck, and
surrounding the truck with a guard of twenty soldiers
with fixed bayonets, accompanied with all the drums and
fifes of the regiment, and a number of officers, Negroes,
and sailors, exhibited him as a spectacle through the principal streets of the town. They fixed a label on the man's
back, on which was written AMERICAN LIBERTY, OR A
SPECIMEN OF DEMOCRACY; and to add to the insult they
played Yankee Doodle: Oh Britain, how art thou fallen!
Is it not enough that British troops, who were once the
terror of France and Spain, should be made the instruments of butchering thy children! But must they descend
also to exploits too infamously dirty for any but the mean-
est of the mob to practice?

By April 1775, Gage, with 3,000 men in Boston and
further reinforcements on the way, felt himself strong
enough to proceed with his instructions to disarm the
resistance and arrest its leaders. On April 18, in the dead
of night, troops were shipped over to Charlestown under
the command of Colonel Smith with instructions to proceed to Concord, to destroy the ammunition and guns
that were stored there, and to arrest revolutionary leaders
who had gone there for meetings of the Massachusetts
Provincial Congress.

How Dr. Joseph Warren and the revolutionary leadership in Boston alerted the people of Massachusetts about
this troop movement by signals in the tower of Old
North Church and by the dispatch of Paul Revere on
horseback is a well-known and oft-told story. When the
first British troops marched into Lexington at daybreak

on their way to Concord, they found the militia, under Captain John Parker, awaiting them. A British officer, as reported by Lieutenant Mackenzie, gave an account of how the troops were ferried from Boston to Charlestown in the dead of night and of what then happened:

The Grenadier and Light Companies of the Regiments in Boston were ordered to assemble on the beach near the magazine at ten o'clock last night [April 18]. The whole was not assembled til near 11; as there were not enough boats to embark them at once, as many as they could contain were embarked, and landed at Phipps's farm. The boats then returned for the remainder, and it was near one o'clock in the morning before the whole were landed on the opposite shore. Two days' provisions which had been dressed on board the transports, were distributed to the troops, at Phipps's farm, which detained them near an hour; so that it was two o'clock before they marched off. Their march across the marshes into the high road, was hasty and fatiguing, and they were obliged to wade, half way up to their thighs, through two inlets, the tide being by that time up. This should have been avoided if possible, as the troops had a long march to perform. In order to make up for the time they had lost, the commanding officer marched at a great rate, till they reached Lexington, where, about daybreak, they found a body of rebels, amounting to about 100 men, drawn up, under arms. They were hastily called to, to disperse. Shots were immediately fired; but from which side could not be ascertained, each party imputing it to the other.

Captain Parker, commanding the Lexington militia, gave his version of the confrontation in a report to the Massachusetts Provincial Congress:

I, John Parker, of lawful age and commander of the militia in Lexington, do testify, and declare, that on the 19th instant, in the morning about one of the clock, being informed . . . that a number of the regular troops were on their march from Boston, in order to take the province stores in Concord, ordered our militia to meet on the common in said Lexington, to consult what to do, and concluded not to be discovered nor meddle with said regular troops (if they should approach) unless they should insult and molest us; and upon their sudden approach, I immediately ordered our militia to disperse and not to fire. Immediately said troops made their appearance and rushing furiously, fired and killed eight of our party, without receiving any provocation therefor from us.

John Robbins, a member of Parker's company, added a more vivid testimony:

There suddenly appeared a number of the King's troops, about a thousand, as I thought, at the distance of about sixty or seventy yards from us, huzzaing, and on a quick pace toward us, with three officers in their front on horseback, and on full gallop toward us, the foremost of which cried, "Throw down your arms, ye villains, ye rebels," upon which said company dispersing, the foremost of the three officers ordered their men, saying "Fire, by God, fire," at which moment we received a very heavy and close fire from them.

The whole countryside was now aroused. Obviously Colonel Smith could not seize the Concord stores without serious resistance. Nonetheless he determined, against the advice of his officers, to go forward with his mission, and arrived at Concord with the troops at about 10:30 A.M. Smith then set a guard on the North and South bridges over the Concord River, which commanded the western approaches to the village, and proceeded to search houses, spike guns, and destroy ammunition. At noon, this mission accomplished, Smith and his men returned to Lexington under brisk fire from the pursuing militia, and there joined the British support troops under the command of Earl Percy. At about 3:15 in the afternoon the whole party, many utterly fatigued and with their ammunition spent, began the long, humiliating sixteen-mile trek back to Boston.

The rebels, a British officer tells us,

always posted themselves in the houses and behind the walls by the roadside, and there waited the approach of the column, when they fired at it. Numbers of them were mounted, and when they had fastened their horses at some little distance from the road, they crept down near enough to have a shot; as soon as the column passed, they mounted again, and rode around until they got ahead of the column, and found some convenient place from whence they might fire again. These fellows were generally good marksmen, and many of them used long guns made for duck shooting.

Lieutenant Mackenzie, who marched with the rear guard, also testified that "numbers of armed men on foot

A LIST of the Names of the PROVINCIALS who were Killed and Wounded in the late Engagement with His Majesty's Troops at *Concord*, &c.

KILLED.

Of *Lexington.*

* Mr. Robert Munroe,
* Mr. Jonas Parker,
* Mr. Samuel Hadley,
* Mr. Jona° Harrington,
* Mr. Caleb Harrington,
* Mr. Isaac Muzzy,
* Mr. John Brown,
Mr. John Raymond,
Mr. Nathaniel Wyman,
Mr. Jedediah Munroe.

Of *Menotomy.*

Mr. Jason Russel,
Mr. Jabez Wyman,
Mr. Jason Winship,

Of *Sudbury.*

Deacon Haynes,
Mr. —— Reed.

Of *Concord.*

Capt. James Miles.

Of *Bedford.*

Capt. Jonathan Willson.

Of *Acton.*

Capt. Davis,
Mr. —— Hosmer,
Mr. James Howard.

Of *Woburn.*

* Mr. Azael Porter,
Mr. Daniel Thompson.

Of *Charlestown.*

Mr. James Miller,
Capt. William Barber's Son.

Of *Brookline.*

Isaac Gardner, Esq;

Of *Cambridge.*

Mr. John Hicks,
Mr. Moses Richardson,
Mr. William Massey.

Of *Medford.*

Mr. Henry Putnam.

Of *Lynn.*

Mr. Abednego Ramsdell,
Mr. Daniel Townsend,
Mr. William Flint,
Mr. Thomas Hadley.

Of *Danvers.*

Mr. Henry Jacobs,
Mr. Samuel Cook,
Mr. Ebenezer Goldthwait,
Mr. George Southwick,
Mr. Benjamin Daland, jun.
Mr. Jotham Webb,
Mr. Perley Putnam.

Of *Salem.*

Mr. Benjamin Peirce.

WOUNDED.

Of *Lexington.*

Mr. John Robbins,
Mr. John Tidd,
Mr. Solomon Peirce,
Mr. Thomas Winship,
Mr. Nathaniel Farmer,
Mr. Joseph Comee,
Mr. Ebenezer Munroe,
Mr. Francis Brown,
Prince Easterbrooks,
(A Negro Man.

Of *Framingham.*

Mr. —— Hemenway.

Of *Bedford.*

Mr. John Lane.

Of *Woburn.*

Mr. George Reed,
Mr. Jacob Bacon.

Of *Medford.*

Mr. William Polly.

Of *Lynn.*

Mr. Joshua Felt,
Mr. Timothy Munroe.

Of *Danvers.*

Mr. Nathan Putnam,
Mr. Dennis Wallis.

Of *Beverly.*

Mr. Nathaniel Cleaves.

MISSING.

Of *Menotomy.*

Mr. Samuel Frost,
Mr. Seth Russell.

Those distinguished with this Mark [*] were killed by the first Fire of the Regulars

Sold in Queen-Street.

and on horseback were continually coming from all parts guided by the firing, and before the column had advanced a mile on the road, we were fired at from all quarters, and particularly from the houses on the roadside and the adjacent stone walls." Some of the soldiers, greatly enraged by the sniping, entered the roadside houses and put to death all the people that they found there. Others entered the houses simply in order to plunder and, as Mackenzie tells us, "were killed in the very act of plundering by those who lay concealed in them."

Since the militia fired only from the cover of trees, walls, or houses, the British could make little defense during the long retreat. "Once they had fired," Mackenzie observed bitterly, "they lay down out of sight until they had loaded again, or the column had passed."

The British lost, by their own estimate, more than seventy killed, and 200 men wounded in action. Long after night had fallen, his Majesty's troops were still trudging painfully along Charlestown Neck to be ferried back to Boston. But they got little rest on their arrival. Thomas Gage, panic-stricken, sent parties out in all directions to work feverishly upon the erection of new gun batteries and fortifications; those who stayed in the barracks nursed their blisters and slept in their clothes. Boston was under siege by the Yankees, who ringed it on all sides; the Revolution had begun.

The new British predicament in Boston and the meaning of the Concord confrontation were neatly expressed in a little song, "The Irishman's Epistle," which became popular as a broadside.

The Irishman's Epistle

By my faith, but I think ye're all makers of bulls,
With your brains in your britches, your bums in your
skulls!
Get home with your muskets and put up your swords,
And look in your books for the meaning of words.
You see now, my honeys, how much you're mistaken,
For Concord by discord can never be taken.

How brave you went out with your muskets all bright,
And thought to be-frighten the folk with the sight;
But when you got there how they powdered your pums
And all the way home how they peppered your bums.
And is it not, honeys, a comical crack
To be proud in the face and shot in the back?

With all of your talkin' and all of your wordin',
And all of your shootin' and marchin' and swordin',
How come you to think now they didn't know how
To be after their firelocks as smartly as you?
You see now, my honeys, 'tis nothing at all,
But to pull at the trigger, and pop goes the ball!

And what have you got now for all your designin',
But a town without vittles to sit down and dine in,
And stare at the floor and scratch at your noodles,
And sing how the Yankees have beaten the Doodles.
I'm sure if you're wise, you'll make peace for a dinner,
For fightin' and fastin' will soon make you thinner.

$\star$ | *5* | $\star$

THE BLAZE OF WAR
Undeclared War, 1775–1776

He has plundered our seas, ravaged our coasts, burnt our towns, and destroyed the lives of our people.

He is, at this time, transporting large armies of foreign mercenaries to complete the works of death, desolation, and tyranny, already begun with circumstances of cruelty and perfidy scarcely paralleled in the most barbarous ages, and totally unworthy the head of a civilized nation.

Declaration of Independence

After Lexington everything changed in a flash. Although war had not been declared, it was now a reality. Royal authority began to disintegrate throughout the colonies, now rapidly, as in Virginia, now slowly, as in New York. Royal governors fled to the protection of British forts and warships, or sailed for England. In colony after colony revolutionary conventions assembled, set up committees to carry forward the day-to-day work of organizing resistance, and began to fashion new systems of government. All over British America the militia began to drill with greater frequency, seriousness, and zest.

In the spring, 1775, the Continental Congress assembled for a second time in Philadelphia. The arrival of the delegates from Massachusetts and Connecticut on May 10 was the occasion for a great demonstration: "They were met," we are told,

about six miles outside the city by the officers of all the companies in the city, and by other gentlemen on horseback, in all amounting to five hundred. When they came within two miles of the city, they were met by a company of riflemen, and a company of infantry, with a band of music, who conducted them through the most public streets of the city to their lodgings, amidst the acclamations of near fifteen thousand spectators.

The most urgent problem that the Congress had to face was that of defense. On June 14 it was resolved to raise an army of 20,000 men; six companies of expert marksmen were to be recruited at once, to form the core of the national force, and to be sent to Boston. These first Continental soldiers were hardy hunters and pioneers who came mainly from the backwoods of Pennsylvania and Virginia. They were enlisted for one year's service, and differed from the militia in two respects: they had to serve their full year and could not, like the militia, drift back home again when the immediate emergency was over; and they could be used *anywhere* within British America that the requirements of war dictated, whereas the militia were organized only for *local* defense —both law and custom forbade their use beyond the confines of the state or region from which they came.

One of these Continental rifle companies was under

Massachuset. Jersey

Riflemen,   *Artillerie*

Continental soldiers sketched in 1781
by Baron Ludwig von Closen.

the command of Michael Cresap, a twenty-eight-year-old Indian fighter from Virginia. Cresap's service to the Revolution was cut short when he died of fever in October 1775, but another man who raised and commanded a rifle company, Daniel Morgan of Frederick County, Virginia, was to become an outstanding commander in the Continental army. He would serve with Benedict Arnold at Quebec and Saratoga, and at the battle of Cowpens in 1781 he would provide a classic demonstration of the proper use of militia in cooperation with professional forces.

The rifles with which these men were armed had barrels over two feet in length, with spiral grooves on the inside to impart a spin to the ball and make it fly true. When handled by practiced marksmen they were weapons of deadly accuracy. As the rifle companies marched to Boston, the people flocked to see the men give exhibitions of their shooting skill. A correspondent for the *Pennsylvania Journal* witnessed such a scene in early August.

These men have been bred in the woods to hardships and dangers from their infancy. They appear as if they were entirely unacquainted with, and had never felt, the passion of fear. With their rifles in their hands, they assume a kind of omnipotence over their enemies. One cannot much wonder at this, when we mention a fact which can be fully attested by several of the reputable persons who were eye-witnesses to it. Two brothers in the company took a piece of board five inches broad and seven inches long, with a bit of white paper, about the size of a dollar, in the center; and while one of them supported this board perpendicularly between his knees, the other, at the distance of upwards of sixty yards, and without any kind of rest, shot eight bullets through it successively, and spared a brother's thigh! Another of the company held a barrel stave perpendicularly in his hands with one edge close to his side, while one of his comrades, at the same distance, and in the same manner before mentioned, shot several bullets through it, without any apprehension of danger on either side. The spectators appearing to be amazed at these feats, were told that upwards of fifty persons in the same company could do the same thing; that there was not one who could not plug nineteen bullets out of twenty, as they termed it, within an inch of the head of a tenpenny nail. . . . Some of them proposed to stand with apples on their heads, while others at the same distance, undertook to shoot them off; but the people who saw the other experiments declined to be witnesses of this. At night a great fire was kindled around a pole planted in the Court House Square, where the company, with the captain at their head, all naked to the waist, and painted like savages . . . indulged a vast concourse of people with a perfect exhibition of a war-dance, and all the maneuvers of Indians, holding council, going to war, circumventing their enemies by defiles, ambuscades, attacking, scalping, etc. It is said by those who are judges that no representation could possibly come nearer the original.

The Continental Congress also appointed a commander-in-chief of all American forces in the field—George

Washington, Esquire, one of the delegates from Virginia. He enters our story June 24, 1775, on the road from Philadelphia to New York, as, dressed in a dark blue military coat with cream-colored facings and large gilt buttons, he rode to take charge of the troops encamped around Boston.

At forty-three years of age Washington had not yet reached the prime of life. He was a huge man, well over six feet tall, an athlete and a fine horseman. He possessed charisma, that indefinable power that some men have to command the love, respect, and loyalty of others, and to inspire them to thought and action. He would exhibit an indomitable will to continue the revolutionary struggle, against apparently insuperable obstacles, difficulties, and discouragements, to the very end.

George Washington was born in 1732, the younger son of a Virginia planter, with no very great expectations of wealth or land as his inheritance. Like many such younger sons, he embarked upon a military career, and in 1755, at the age of twenty-three, he was appointed commander-in-chief of all Virginia forces recruited for action in the French and Indian Wars. He was with Braddock that same year in the disastrous defeat at Fort Duquesne. When he retired from the military service in 1759 he had made a reputation for himself as an energetic organizer and a capable leader.

Washington's fortunes changed when he married an heiress, Martha Custis, in 1759, and when, as the result of the death of his brother's widow two years later, he came into possession of the family estate at Mount Vernon on the Potomac. Washington now settled down to a planter's life and devoted himself, until the outbreak of the Revolution, with single-minded zeal to the business of advancing his own fortunes. By 1775 he was the owner of 30,000 acres of Virginia and Ohio lands, a delegate from Fairfax County to the Virginia House of Burgesses, and a successful and respected member of the planter aristocracy. America's foremost freedom fighter was also the owner of 135 black slaves.

In 1775 the British also appointed a new commander-in-chief, to replace the timid and indecisive Thomas Gage. General Sir William Howe (known to his friends as Billy) arrived in Boston on May 25 on board the man o' war *Cerberus* and took over his new command in August. Like Washington, Howe had fought in the French and Indian Wars side by side with the Americans. With Wolfe he had stormed Quebec in 1759, and his reputation was that of a brilliant and gallant officer. Howe and his older brother, Admiral Richard Howe who assumed naval command in America in 1776, were in sympathy with the colonists, and distinctly opposed to their government's warlike policy. Both men cordially loathed Lord Germain, British Secretary of State for War; as a matter of fact, neither brother was on speaking terms with the man in charge of directing Britain's war effort.

Along with Billy Howe on the *Cerberus* there arrived two other gentlemen who were to play an important part in the revolutionary war, and whom we shall meet again later: General Sir John Burgoyne (known to his friends and foes as "Gentleman Johnny") and General Sir Henry Clinton. This new command group was at once dubbed the "junto" by the disrespectful Yankees. Its mission, as everyone realized, was to put an end to rebellion by fire and sword. The American mood, mingling defiance and contempt, is well conveyed by the "Junto Song," which appeared in June and was soon a number-one hit.

Junto Song

turn his coat, And mon - ey __ we must raise, And a - tax - ing we will go, will go, And a - tax - ing we will go.

One single thing untaxed at home,
  Old England could not show,
For money we abroad did roam,
  And thought to tax the *New*,
CHORUS

The power supreme of Parliament
　　Our purpose did assist,
And taxing laws abroad were sent,
　　Which rebels do resist,
CHORUS

Shall we not make the rascals bend
　　To Britain's supreme power?
The sword shall we not to them send,
　　And leaden balls a shower?
CHORUS

Boston we shall in ashes lay,
　　It is a nest of knaves,
We'll make them soon for mercy pray,
　　Or send them to their graves,
CHORUS

We'll force and fraud in one unite
　　To bring them to our hands,
Then lay a tax on the sun's light
　　And a king's tax on their lands,
CHORUS

The first action undertaken by the "junto" was to attack Bunker Hill, on the Charlestown Peninsula overlooking Boston, after the Yankees had seized it for use as a bastion from which to bombard the town. The British soldiers stormed the heights on June 17 with great courage in the face of withering fire, and drove the militia out. But they suffered brutal losses—1,000 men dead or disabled out of 2,400 engaged. Where would replacements come from to fight such a war as this, as the conflict widened, as it became ever clearer that revolution could not be stopped simply by sending in small "punitive" expeditions?

*Lieutenant Grosvenor of Framingham, Massachusetts,
and his slave Peter Salem, both of whom fought at
Bunker Hill. A detail from "The Battle of Bunker Hill,"
by John Trumbull (1765-1843).*

In solving this problem the hands of the government in London were to some extent tied. There was a long-standing tradition in England that forbade the "pressing" of men by compulsory draft for overseas service. The English people throughout their history had never taken up arms in large numbers unless the British Isles themselves were menaced by invasion. "Selective service," in other words, was regarded as a basic English right. The trouble, from the government's point of view, was that the people, *not* their rulers, had the right of selecting the wars that they would, or would not, take part in.

Obviously the Americans were not engaged in an invasion of the British Isles, and therefore there was absolutely no hope of recruiting large numbers of young Englishmen for an anti-American war. Indeed, the absence of whole-hearted support for the war effort among the English people is a striking fact of the Revolution. Peter Van Schaak, a New York loyalist who fled to England in 1776, wrote that "vast numbers" of Englishmen were pro-American. "The people at large," he said, "love the Americans."

Lord George Germain therefore had to look for other solutions to his problem. To some extent he filled the ranks of his armies with the British poor—destitute and landless peasants from the Irish bogs and the Scottish highlands, the sweepings of the London streets and the scourings of the jails. And next he turned to the use of mercenaries, hired soldiers from the German provinces of Hanover, Hesse, and Brunswick. "Ten thousand Hanoverians," the *Constitutional Gazette* reported on September 30, 1775,

A cartoon of a Hessian grenadier,
by an unknown artist, 1778.

are to be taken into British pay, the expenses to be defrayed out of duties to be laid by Parliament, and levied in America. . . . Every Hanoverian soldier who shall have served seven years with the approval of his superior officer or officers, shall have a portion of ground, not more than fifty nor less than twenty acres, rent free, forever.

Finally, and most important, the British government calculated that *Americans themselves* would provide the rank and file of the army that would subdue America. Loyalists, or Tories as they were sometimes called, were simply those people who, for whatever reasons, sided with the British. They were to be found in all sections of the country, among both the rich and the poor, but it is impossible to estimate how many of them there were. There must have been, from first to last, tens of thousands of such people, many of whom actually took up arms for the British cause.

The first clear statement of British policy toward loyalists was made by the Earl of Dunmore, governor of Virginia. When the Revolution broke out, Dunmore fled to a British warship, the H.M.S. *William*, anchored off Norfolk. On November 7, 1775, he issued an important proclamation: "I have thought fit," wrote His Lordship,

to issue this, my proclamation, hereby declaring [that] I do, in virtue of the power and authority to me given by his Majesty, determine to execute martial law, and cause the same to be executed throughout this colony; and to the end that peace and good order may the sooner be restored, I do require every person capable of bearing arms to resort to his Majesty's STANDARD, or be looked upon as a traitor to his crown and government, and thereby become liable to the penalty the law inflicts for such offenses, such as forfeiture of life, confiscation of lands, etc. etc.

Then came a shrewd blow. Dunmore emancipated the bondsmen and slaves. "I do further declare," he wrote, "all indentured servants, Negroes, or others, appertaining to rebels, FREE, that are willing and able to bear arms, they joining his Majesty's troops, as soon as may be, for the purpose of reducing this colony to a proper sense of their duty to his Majesty's crown and dignity."

Here, evidently, lay the biggest potential supply of recruits for the loyalist cause. We must not forget that at the time of the Revolution there were not only hundreds of thousands of slaves in the colonies, primarily among the southern states, but also many indentured servants, particularly in New York, Pennsylvania, and Virginia. Indentured servants were white laborers bound to serve their masters for a stated term of years. Their position was not easily distinguishable from that of the black slaves. Many of these oppressed people, both white and black, were sorely tempted to join the British if by so doing they might gain their freedom. Take, for example, this advertisement for a runaway that appeared in the *Pennsylvania Journal* on March 4, 1777:

Ran away from Isaac Harris, living in Pittsgrove, Salem County, Pennsylvania, an English servant man, named William Blackmore; about twenty-two years of age; five feet five, or six inches high; light of complexion, light straight hair; a very clumsy fellow, turns the toe of his right foot very much out in his walk; very much addicted to swearing and getting drunk; he has run away several times, and has an iron collar around his neck, marked I.H. and W.B., which he wears under his shirt, but may be easily discovered. Had on, when he went away, a brown cloth coat with blue sleeves, a light colored cloth jacket, leather britches and blue stockings. . . . He will endeavor to get to the [British] army if he has an opportunity, as he is a great Tory. [Emphasis added.]

Dunmore did not get an opportunity to recruit in earnest. A month after his proclamation, on December 9, his forces—some half of whom were runaway slaves— were defeated at Great Bridge by the Virginia militia and obliged to flee back to the ships. On January 1, 1776, the governor took his revenge by bombarding Norfolk and reducing it to ashes. On that day, the *Pennsylvania Evening Post* reported:

The British fleet commenced a cannonade against the town, from upwards of one hundred pieces of cannon, and continued til nearly ten o'clock at night, without intermission. Under cover of their guns the Regulars landed and set fire to the town in several places. . . . The houses being chiefly of wood, took fire immediately, and the fire spread with amazing rapidity. It is now become general, and the whole town will probably be consumed in a day or two.

British naval operations in 1775 were not confined to the Norfolk area; the fleet brought terror to the entire

American coast with its sudden attacks and furious bombardments. A correspondent of the *Constitutional Gazette* wrote from Annapolis on September 18:

We are much astonished at the behavior of some of those captains of men o' war, who are stationed on our coasts. They seem greedily to anticipate the horror of bloodshedding; and although war is not yet proclaimed, nor any hostilities ordered by Parliament against the colonies in general, yet confiding in their strength, they daringly assault our towns and destroy lives upon the least provocation whatever.

On October 7 a British flotilla appeared off Bristol Harbor, in Narragansett Bay, and began to bombard the town in order to persuade the inhabitants to comply with a demand for 200 sheep and 30 cattle. One casualty of this encounter was the Reverend John Burt, who, sick in bed when the attack began, "left his habitation to seek some place of safety, and was [the following day] found dead in a neighboring field."

After the destruction of Falmouth, Massachusetts, on October 18 by a similar attack, a number of New England coastal towns were vacated by the inhabitants. "Nearly all the people belonging to Cape Ann," reported the *New England Chronicle* on November 2, "have evacuated the town, and have proceeded so far in removing their effects, as to take away the glass windows from the meeting house and many of the dwelling houses."

These acts of war provoked sobering reflections. The British, wrote "An American" in the *Virginia Gazette*, "have done their worst; and to no other purpose, than to harden our soldiers, and teach them to bear without dismay, all the most formidable operations of a war carried on by a powerful and cruel enemy; to no other purpose, than to give the world specimens of British cruelty and American fortitude."

The fear of British attack and the mood of resistance that swept the country after Lexington gripped the southern colonists too. In June 1775 the Provincial Congress of South Carolina met in the beautiful and stately capital of Charleston, and set up the Council of Safety to organize defense. All the members of the council were leaders of South Carolina society, and not a few of them had been educated in England.

The council set to work to raise three regiments of militia to defend the town, and a regiment of artillery. Ships were sent out to the West Indies to purchase gunpowder, which was in desperately short supply, and one fast sloop was dispatched with the mission of seizing 17,000 pounds of powder from a British ship at St. Augustine. In a little while tents began to bloom on James Island, where some of the troops were stationed, at the southeastern edge of Charleston Harbor. Colonel William Moultrie, one of the regimental commanders, wrote:

We now began to look like soldiers, and kept up a strict discipline. The men were taught the manual [of arms], and the exercise of the great guns, which made them matrosses [gunners] as well as infantry; they were as well clothed as troops could be, and made a handsome appearance; we thought it best to form our camp on James' Island, for the benefit of the soldiers' health, and the better

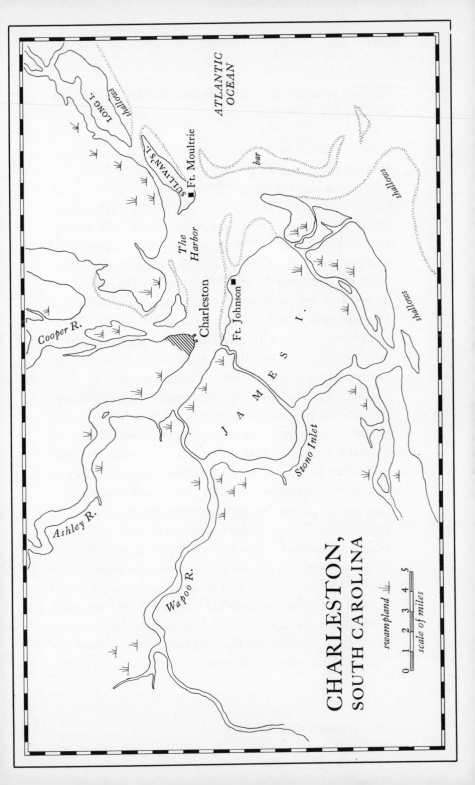

ATLANTIC
OCEAN

LONG I.

shalloos

SULLIVAN'S I.

■ Ft. Moultrie

bar

shalloes

shalloes

The Harbor

Charleston

■ Ft. Johnson

J A M E S I.

Cooper R.

Stono Inlet

Ashley R.

Wapoo R.

CHARLESTON,
SOUTH CAROLINA

swampland

0 1 2 3 4 5
scale of miles

situated to keep them from liquor, which it was impossible to do in Charleston.

At the same time the council made frantic preparations to put the gun batteries in order, which they relied on for the defense of the town. "We were very fortunate," wrote Colonel Moultrie, "in having a great number of large cannon, and a great number of balls suitable in the King's arsenal." But many of the gun carriages were rotten, and new ones had to be made. The work went on fast enough, said Moultrie, "as the mechanics almost to a man were hearty in the cause and went cheerfully to work whenever they were called upon." These "mechanics" were white craftsmen who not only worked on the guns, but put the forts in repair and provided clothes, equipment, and boats for the troops.

Charleston may have been enthusiastic about defense, but this was not necessarily true of the people in the back country: many were Regulators who felt deep resentment against the slave-owning rulers in the lowlands and were not particularly disposed to join them in their struggle. Therefore the Council of Safety organized a military expedition to patrol the back country. Since, as Moultrie pointed out, "some of the people there were still unsettled in their minds with respect to the Revolution, and some opposed directly to it," a show of military force might "fix the wavering and intimidate the disaffected."

Most of the heavy, unskilled labor in the defense preparations was performed by black slaves hired by the council from their owners and brought into town from the estates in the countryside around. After Dunmore's proclamation liberating the slaves (November 1775) the patriot leaders became very nervous. British frigates constantly hovered off the Charleston coast; the defenders of the city became convinced that a plot was afoot in the British navy to seize Sullivan's Island and use it as a recruiting base for fugitives. The British, Moultrie wrote, were busy "enticing our Negroes to run away and form a camp on Sullivan's Island; we were informed that nearly 500 had already encamped there. This was very alarming, and looked on as dangerous to the province at large; and that it was absolutely necessary at all events to dislodge them from this place."

Sullivan's Island, on the northeastern side of the harbor, was a wilderness of live oak, palmetto, and myrtle facing out across the pounding breakers of the Atlantic and separated from the mainland by a channel of water about a mile wide. The Council of Safety made a landing on the island in the middle of December 1775. It found no runaways there, but began the construction of a fort and stationed forces there with the mission "to fire upon any ships of war, boats or other vessels belonging to the enemy attempting to approach, pass or land troops upon the island." In March the council appointed Moultrie as commander of the Sullivan's Island garrison; work on the fort continued through the first six months of 1776. As this bastion "was looked upon as the key to the harbor," Moultrie wrote, "a great number of mechanics and Negro laborers were employed in finishing [it] as fast as possible."

The American experts had little confidence in Moultrie and his fort, which wasn't even built of stone, but only of palmetto logs. General Charles Lee, who had been sent down from Philadelphia to assume overall command of the troops in the Charleston area, was not impressed with the easy-going Moultrie and his southern militia. And one sea captain, who had seen service with the British, predicted, in no uncertain terms, that when the imperial navy "come to lay alongside your fort, they will knock it down in half an hour." This did not seem to bother Moultrie, who replied calmly that if that was the case, "we will lay behind the ruins and prevent their men from landing."

On June 1, 1776, a British fleet finally appeared off Charleston, under the combined command of Sir Henry Clinton and Admiral Sir Peter Parker. The British plan was to land soldiers on Long Island, directly north of Sullivan's Island, and then to launch a combined attack on Fort Moultrie by land and by sea—the naval guns bombarding the fort while Clinton's men forded the ditch between the two islands and moved down from the north by land. The original objective of the British expedition had been North Carolina, where Clinton hoped to recruit many fighters from among the Scots, Highlanders, and Regulators of that region; but unforeseen obstacles had foiled this plan. The attack on Sullivan's Island was a consolation prize that had a great appeal. It could be done quickly, with time enough to get the main British force back to New York for the summer campaign; and it would provide an ideal base from which to organize an army of black runaways from the swarming lowland plantations.

British preparations were complete by the end of June,

General Charles Lee,
from an engraving by
A. H. Ritchie (1822-1895).

and the attack began June 28. At 10 A.M. the fleet—the *Bristol,* Sir Peter Parker's flagship (50 guns); the *Experiment* (50); the *Active* (28); the *Solebay* (28); the *Syren* (28); the *Actaeon* (28); the *Sphinx* (28); and the *Friendship* (26)—sailed up to the fort and began bombarding it.

The cannonade continued all day and well into the evening, but Moultrie lost only ten men killed and a few wounded. The British suffered severely from the American fire, with over a hundred seamen killed and many wounded. Worst of all, Sir Henry Clinton took absolutely no part in the engagement: he found that the water between Long and Sullivan's islands was too deep for his men to ford, and he was obliged to look on from a distance, a helpless spectator.

There were other spectators, too. "During the action," Moultrie recalled, "thousands of our fellow citizens were looking on with anxious hopes and fears, some of whom had fathers, brothers, and husbands in the battle; whose hearts must have been pierced by every broadside. After some time our flag was shot away; their hopes were then gone, and they gave up all for lost." But a sergeant retrieved the flag in spite of heavy fire, and raised it again on the ramparts, so that "our flag once more waving in the air, revived the drooping spirits of our friends; and they continued looking on, til night had closed the scene, and hid us from their view."

Then the British gave up the fight and slipped away, leaving behind the *Actaeon,* which had run aground. Next day it blew up and, Moultrie reported, "from the explosion issued a grand pillar of smoke, which soon expanded itself at the top, and to appearance formed the figure of a palmetto tree; the ship immediately burst into a great blaze that continued till she burnt down to the water's edge."

An officer with the British fleet wrote of the engagement on September 14: "I can scarcely believe what I saw on that day; a day to me one of the most distressing of my life. The navy on this occasion behaved with their usual coolness and intrepidity. One would have imagined that no battery could have resisted their incessant fire."

Even more surprised than the British at Moultrie's victory was the American commander himself, General Lee, who at once lost his reserve toward the militia colonel and, as Moultrie recalled, "made me his bosom friend." All over British America people rocked with laughter when they heard that Sir Peter Parker had had his pants blown off during the engagement. Everyone began singing a little ditty in which the admiral plaintively reports the engagement to his superiors.

English pistol used in the revolutionary wars.

Sir Peter Parker

Voice

G   C

My

(Guitar Instrumental)

Lords, by your leave,   An ac-count I will give   That de-

Dmi.

serves   to be writ-ten   in   met-er.   For the

G   C

reb-els   and   I   Have been pret-ty   nigh,   Faith,

C   Dmi.   D⁷

al - most too nigh for Sir Pe - ter.   Ti - mi

al - der-ry O,   Ti - mi al - der - ry day,   Faith,

al - most too nigh for Sir Pe - ter!

With much labor and toil
Unto Sullivan's Isle,
I came firm as Falstaff or Pistol;
But the Yankees, God rot 'em,
I could not get at 'em,
They most terribly mauled my poor *Bristol*.

CHORUS

The Blaze of War 113

Bold Clinton by land
Did quietly stand,
While I made a thundering clatter.
But the channel was deep,
So he only could peep
And not venture over the water.

CHORUS

Devil take 'em, their shot
Came so swift and so hot,
And the cowardly dogs stood so stiff, sirs!
That I put ship about
And was glad to get out
Or they would not have left me a skiff, sirs!

CHORUS

Now, bold as a Turk,
I proceed to New York,
Where with Clinton and Howe you may find me.
I've the wind in my tail, and am hoisting sail,
To leave Sullivan's Island behind me.

CHORUS

But, my lords, do not fear,
For before the next year,
Although a small island could fret us,
The continent whole
We shall take, by my soul,
If the cowardly Yankees will let us.

CHORUS

☆ *6* ☆

INDEPENDENCE
Common Sense *and Continental Union,* 1776

Prudence, indeed, will dictate that governments long estab-lished should not be changed for light and transient causes; and accordingly all experience hath shown, that mankind are more disposed to suffer, while evils are sufferable, than to right themselves by abolishing the forms to which they are accustomed. But when a long train of abuses and usurpations, pursuing invariably the same object, evinces a design to reduce them under absolute despotism, it is their right, it is their duty, to throw off such government, and to provide new guards for their future security.

Declaration of Independence

By the end of 1775 it was clear that Great Britain and her American colonies were at war. Blood had been shed in direct encounters between colonial and imperial troops at Lexington, Concord, and Bunker Hill. Boston was not only under British military occupation—as it had been, to be sure, ever since 1768—but was also besieged by an all-American army, whose commander-in-chief, George Washington, had his headquarters at Harvard College, in the village of Cambridge. American coastal towns awaited daily with dread the appearance of the British fleet in their waters, the landing of raiding parties, the bombardment of their houses and docks.

Under the pressure of these events Americans were moving closer to the acceptance of an idea that at an earlier time they would have rejected with horror: that separation from Great Britain and the creation of American independence were inevitable and desirable. This new public mood began to crystallize rapidly in the first months of 1776 under the impact of *Common Sense,* one of the most widely read and influential writings ever produced in this country. Its author, Tom Paine, was a penniless English needleworker who had been in America little more than one year before the appearance of his pamphlet made him famous.

Thomas Paine was born in 1737 in the obscure little village of Thetford in England's eastern county of Norfolk. Set to work while still a child, Paine moved from job to job and led an unhappy, poverty-stricken life that had no fixed or settled goal. Finally in 1774, dispirited, unhappy in his marriage, and out of work, he decided to emigrate. He went to London to see Benjamin Franklin, Pennsylvania's agent in the capital, and asked him for a letter of recommendation. Thus armed he arrived in Philadelphia in November 1774, found work, and began to earn his living by helping to publish a new journal, the *Pennsylvania Magazine.* Paine was at this time thirty-eight years old: he found, to his astonishment, that the country was in the midst of revolution.

Before Lexington and Concord, Paine shared, with so many others, the belief that America's quarrel with England would be patched up and that all would end with an amicable settlement. He recalled in later years that early in 1775 the people's attachment to Great Britain was firm: "It was at that time a kind of treason to speak against it. They disliked the ministry, but they esteemed the nation. Their idea of a grievance operated without resentment; and their single object was reconciliation."

But as the year unfolded and blood was shed, Paine's opinions began to change. A poor craftworker, he had brought with him to America a blazing hatred for the British aristocracy with its wealth, its cruel treatment of the common people, and its disdain for them. Now he found in the New World the same tyranny from which he had fled in the Old. In this situation he discovered in himself talents that he had until now been unaware of, and began to put them to use. These gifts, he recalled, "were buried in me, and might ever have continued so, had not the necessity of the times dragged and driven them into action."

Late in 1775 Paine began to set his thoughts down on paper, and *Common Sense* was published in Philadelphia early in January 1776. One of the most brilliant among many fine American revolutionary propagandists had made his first public appearance.

Paine stated his new convictions in bold and incisive terms. "Everything," he cried, "that is right or natural pleads for separation. The blood of the slain, the weeping voice of nature cries, *'Tis time to part*." No man, he continued, had wished more deeply than he for reconciliation with Great Britain and its royal authority before the fatal day of April 19, 1775. When that event became known, "I rejected the hardened, sullen-tempered Pharaoh of England forever."

The American cause, said Paine, is a righteous one:

The sun never shined on a cause of greater worth. 'Tis not the affair of a city, a county, a province, or a kingdom, but of a continent—of at least one eighth part of the habitable globe. 'Tis not the concern of a day, a year, or an age; posterity are virtually involved in the contest, and will be more or less affected, even to the end of time, by the proceedings now. Now is the seed-time of continental union, faith, and honor. The least fracture now will be like a name engraved with the point of a pin on the tender rind of a young oak; the wood will enlarge with the tree, and posterity read it in full-grown characters.

Paine proceeded to examine the objections of those—and there were many—who might still doubt his conclusions. Britain, you say, is the parent country: Is it not disgraceful to revolt against the parent who has nurtured you; is not this the shameful ingratitude of a thankless child? Not so, Paine answered; if England is our parent, "then the more shame upon her conduct. Even brutes do not devour their young, nor savages make war upon their families; wherefore the assertion, if true, turns to her reproach."

But, he continued, the assertion—that Britain was the parent country—is not true, or at best, only partly true. "Europe, not England, is the parent country of America. This new world hath been the asylum for the persecuted lovers of civil and religious liberty from every part of Europe. Hither have they fled, not from the tender embraces of the mother, but from the cruelty of the monster; and it is so far true of England, that the same tyranny which drove the first emigrants from home, pursues their descendants still."

The doubters are not yet satisfied. "Come," they say, "this is only a family quarrel. It will be patched up; we shall be friends again for all this." Paine asked: Is such a thing really possible? Examine the situation: blood has been shed, men have died, towns have been raided, houses and property destroyed. If you tell me that we can overlook this,

Then I ask, hath your house been burnt? Hath your property been destroyed before your face? Are your wife and children destitute of a bed to lie on, or bread to live on? Have you lost a parent or a child by their hands, and yourself the ruined and wretched survivor? If you have not, then are you not a judge for those who have. But if you have, and can still shake hands with the murderers, then you are unworthy the name of husband, father, friend, or lover, and whatever may be your rank or title in life, you have the heart of a coward, and the spirit of a sycophant.

The time had passed, Paine concluded, when the American nation could be governed from Europe. "There was a time when it was proper, and there is a proper time for it to cease." The time, he said, is now; and he ended with this burning appeal:

O ye that love mankind! Ye that dare oppose, not only the tyranny, but the tyrant, stand forth! Every spot of

the old world is overrun with oppression. Freedom hath been hunted round the globe. Asia, and Africa, have long expelled her. Europe regards her like a stranger, and England hath given her warning to depart. O! receive the fugitive, and prepare in time an asylum for mankind.

Common Sense was well received by the public. Independence became a subject of controversy as dog-eared copies of the pamphlet were passed from hand to hand, talked about, written about, and quoted in the press. The *Constitutional Gazette* stated the situation precisely when it observed on February 24, 1776:

This animated piece dispels, with irresistible energy, the prejudice of the mind against the doctrine of independence, and pours in upon it such an inundation of light and truth, as will produce an instantaneous and marvelous change in the temper, in the views and feelings of an American. The ineffable delight with which it is perused, and its doctrines imbibed, is a demonstration that the seeds of independence, though imported with the troops from Britain, will grow surprisingly with proper cultivation in the fields of America.

Supported and moved forward by the changing tide of opinion, the colonies now began, one by one, to set up their own systems of government and to prepare constitutions under which those governments should be conducted. In May 1776 a revolutionary convention assembled at Williamsburg to draft a constitution for the state of Virginia. This convention also instructed the Virginia delegates to the Continental Congress to request the

Congress "to declare the united colonies free and independent states, absolved from all allegiance or dependence on the Crown or Parliament of Great Britain."

On June 7, Richard Henry Lee, a Virginia delegate to the Continental Congress, submitted a resolution to that body in accordance with the instructions he had received:

RESOLVED, *that these United Colonies are, and of right ought to be, free and independent states, that they are absolved from all allegiance to the British Crown, and that all political connection between them and the State of Great Britain is, and ought to be, totally dissolved.*

Lee's introduction of this resolution sparked a sharp debate. Some delegates protested that it was too soon to declare for independence and that the people of the middle colonies "were not yet ripe for bidding adieu to the British connection." Others argued that separation from Great Britain was now a *fact*; that it was only necessary to recognize it; and that the Congress must not wait longer, but must give the country a bold lead.

Finally a compromise was agreed upon. It was decided to postpone action on the Lee resolution until July 1 to permit support to ripen in the middle colonies, that is, in New York, New Jersey, Pennsylvania, Delaware, and Maryland. In the meantime Congress set up a committee of five members to draft a Declaration of Independence. Thomas Jefferson, who had taken his seat as a Virginia delegate to the Continental Congress in 1775, was one of these. The others were John Adams (Massachusetts), Benjamin Franklin (Pennsylvania), Roger Sherman (Connecticut), and Robert R. Livingston (New York).

These gentlemen then requested Jefferson to prepare the draft.

Jefferson, who had a reputation as a skilled pamphleteer, set to work and prepared a statement that was approved by the committee with only minor changes; this was submitted to Congress on June 28, a little more than two weeks later. Congress proceeded to debate the Lee resolution on July 1, and passed it the next day. They then examined Jefferson's draft of the Declaration of Independence, made substantial revisions in it, and adopted the revised Declaration on July 4, 1776.

What was the purpose of Jefferson's Declaration? Would it not have been sufficient to have passed the Lee resolution, and simply to have declared, as a matter of fact, that the colonies were now "free and independent states"?

There were many reasons why such a step would have been insufficient. Revolution is a serious business. It means that you take up arms against the constituted government, and seek to overthrow it with the use of force and violence. There is loss of life, human anguish, the destruction of property, with the ensuing suffering and distress. Clearly it is no light matter to ask people to embark on this course; hence the need, through the Declaration, to justify it morally in the eyes of the nation and of the world. Such was the purpose of the first part of the Declaration, in which Jefferson wrote:

When in the course of human events it becomes necessary for one people to dissolve the political bands which have connected them with another, and to assume among the powers of the earth, the separate and equal station to which the laws of nature and of nature's God entitle them, a decent respect to the opinions of mankind requires that they should declare the causes which impel them to separation.

The causes of this separation, as Jefferson explained them, were simple enough: the British government had ceased to protect the American people in their God-given rights to life, liberty, and the pursuit of happiness, and had turned, after 1763, into a tyrannical monster trampling these rights underfoot. The people therefore had a right, even a duty, to abolish this evil government and to make other arrangements for their security. And, if they could not abolish the wicked government in any other way, clearly they would have the right to use force.

Here a difficulty presents itself. Jefferson was himself a slave owner at the very moment he penned the brave words, *We hold these truths to be self-evident, that all men are created equal, that they are endowed by their Creator with certain inalienable rights, that among these are life, liberty, and the pursuit of happiness.* Was he, then, guilty of hypocrisy? If he held slaves himself, could he really be sincere in asserting that all men must enjoy equal rights, including an equal right to freedom?

Later on slave owners would get around the Declaration by arguing that slaves were not men, but an inferior species, and that in any event they were not intended to be included in the American community by the words of the Declaration. Jefferson never took this obviously racist position. He knew that slaves were men, and he insisted that they were entitled to their freedom as much as any other man. The proof of this is found in the original draft of the Declaration, in which Jefferson had included a passionate denunciation of slavery and the slave trade. The king, he charged, in permitting trading companies to import Africans to America,

has waged cruel war against human nature itself, violating its most sacred rights of life and liberty in the persons of a distant people who never offended him, capturing and carrying them into slavery in another hemisphere, or to incur miserable death in their transportation thither.

Much to Jefferson's disgust this denunciation of slavery was stricken from the final draft of the Declaration, primarily at the insistence of the delegates from Georgia and South Carolina. Even so, these words remain graven in the historical record. They show that Jefferson believed in the rights of black men and that he was, indeed, the first American statesman of the first rank to give open, public expression to his belief. He understood clearly, and recorded the fact, that slavery in a free country is a gross and dangerous anomaly. He condemned it in no uncertain terms, and called for its abolition.

Recognition of this fact only opens up another difficulty. Not only was Jefferson a slave owner when he wrote the Declaration, but he remained so until the end of his life—and he lived a long time, not dying until 1824, or nearly fifty years after penning the Declaration. If Jefferson *really* believed that slavery was wrong and that black men, like all other men, had a right to free-

Cain and Abel, from a
Pennsylvania Dutch cast-iron stove
made in 1741.

dom—if he believed this, why then did he not free his own slaves?

It will not do to argue, as some have done, that Jefferson was a kind master and that he treated his black people well. Kindness is no substitute for freedom; sad to say, even kind masters could be guilty of brutality, and even here Jefferson was no exception. Take for example, the case of Jame Hubbard, who ran away from Jefferson several times. In 1812 Jefferson had Jame, as he himself wrote, "severely flogged in the presence of his old companions," and then sold him. The purpose of the flogging was to warn the other "boys" what would happen to them if they too got the idea that they were entitled to their freedom.

Thomas Jefferson did believe that his slaves had a right to freedom; but he thought of them as Africans, not as Americans. To him, as to most whites in that day, it was unthinkable that free black men should have the right to mingle on an equal footing with white people. No, if they were to enjoy freedom, they must be sent back to Africa. But, posed in these terms, Jefferson's problem was insoluble. The return of half a million black people to Africa would require a colossal outlay of funds. Who would pay for it? Certainly not Thomas Jefferson—as a matter of fact, he remained in debt until the end of his life. The lot of the free Negro in America —despised, outcast, and oppressed—was an unenviable one. Jefferson might be pardoned for the conclusion that, if the alternative was to keep his slaves or simply turn them loose, the former choice was the more kindly one.

The Declaration of Independence ended with a formal announcement that a new nation had come into being. "We . . . solemnly publish and declare," said Congress, "that these united colonies are and of right ought to be free and independent states; that they are absolved from all allegiance to the British Crown, and that all political connection between them and the State of Great Britain is, and ought to be, totally dissolved." This left the way open for other countries to accord legal recognition to the United States government, to enter into alliance with it, and to offer it military and financial aid.

The Declaration was received with ceremony and rejoicing throughout the colonies. In Philadelphia the document was read on July 8 to a vast concourse of the inhabitants at the State House. The *Pennsylvania Evening Post* reported that at Easton, Pennsylvania, on July 11:

The Colonel and all the other field officers of the first battalion repaired to the court-house, the light infantry company marching there with their drums beating, fifes playing, and the standard, the device for which is the thirteen United Colonies, which was ordered to be displayed. After that the Declaration was read aloud to a great number of spectators, who gave their hearty assent with three loud huzzas, and cried out, "May God preserve long and unite the Free and Independent States of America."

In Princeton, New Jersey, the town hall was "grandly illuminated," an observer tells us, "and INDEPENDENCY proclaimed under a triple volley of musketry" on July 9.

The following day the Declaration was read in New York City to all the brigades of the Continental army. "It was received," we are told, "with loud huzzas, and the utmost demonstrations of joy."

In Massachusetts the Declaration was proclaimed from the Town House in Boston "amidst the acclamations of thousands, who assembled on the occasion." In Rhode Island on July 20 the brigade of Continental troops stationed at the capital, Newport, marched to the State House and drew up on parade. The *Pennsylvania Evening Post* reported:

His honor the Governor and the members of the Assembly then marched through and received the compliments of the brigade . . . The Declaration was then read; next thirteen cannon were discharged at Fort Liberty, and then the brigade drew up and fired in thirteen divisions, from east to west, agreeable to the number and situation of the United States. The Declaration was received with joy and applause in by all ranks.

News of the Declaration did not reach Georgia until August. On the tenth of that month the president and council of the state at Savannah, recorded the *Pennsylvania Evening Post,*

proceeded to the square before the assembly house, and read [the Declaration] to a great concourse of people, when the grenadier and light infantry companies fired a general volley. After this they proceeded [in procession] to the liberty pole: the grenadiers in front; the provost-marshal, on horseback, with his sword drawn; the secre-

tary, with the Declaration; his Excellency, the President; the honorable the council, and the gentlemen attending; then the light infantry and the rest of the militia of the town and district of Savannah. At the Liberty-pole they were met by the Georgia battalion, who, after the reading of the Declaration, discharged their field-pieces, and fired in platoons. Upon this they proceeded to the battery, at the trustee's gardens, where the Declaration was read for the last time, and the cannon of the battery discharged.

☆ | 7 | ☆

THE TRUMPET OF A PROPHECY
New York and New Jersey Campaigns, 1776–1777

Be my words
To unawakened earth, the trumpet of a prophecy
Percy Bysshe Shelley, "Ode to the West Wind"

The city of New York was one of America's largest ports, set amid surroundings of extraordinary beauty and grandeur. It was located at the very tip of Manhattan Island, which stretched away for fourteen miles to the north amid peaceful farms and wooded rocky heights. The city's lovely harbor, the key to its prosperity and wealth, lay below the town, bounded by the New Jersey coast on the west, the sandy shore of Staten Island on the south, and Paumanok (Long Island) on the east. "On both sides of the harbor," wrote a Scots traveler, Patrick M'Robert, in August 1774, "the woods, country houses, orchards, and fields of Indian corn form at this season of the year a beautiful prospect. There is very good water up to [the city], the harbor is spacious and large, with many convenient docks or quays, with storehouses upon them for vessels of any burden to lie always afloat alongside of them."

Until the summer of 1776 New York had been spared the horrors of war; but now its turn had come. When we were exploring the undeclared war in 1775–1776, we left George Washington, the New England militia, and the Continental forces sitting in a ring around Shawmut, besieging the British in Boston. As the siege dragged on, Billy Howe began to realize that he could not win— the revolutionary movement in New England was too strong. Would it not be wise, he asked himself, to find a more secure base for operations against the rebellion?

New York naturally suggested itself. It provided an ideal harbor in the midst of a wealthy agricultural country, and the people, by all accounts, were not as "disaffected" as the Yankees. In addition, New York was the southern anchor of the great Hudson-Champlain waterway, stretching from the Gulf of St. Lawrence southward to the Atlantic and navigable by ocean-going ships for two-thirds of the distance. Effective control of this water route would seal off New England from the rest of the colonies and enable the British to subdue the rebellion piecemeal.

That the seizure of the Hudson Valley route would mark the beginning of the end for the Revolution was obvious to the Americans as well as to Howe. The first military act of the patriots after Lexington was the seizure of Forts Ticonderoga and Crown Point in May 1775 by a party of New England militia headed by Ethan Allen of Vermont. Hard upon the heels of this success Washington authorized an invasion of the St. Lawrence Valley under the direction of his two most fearless field commanders, Richard Montgomery and Benedict Arnold. The objective was to drive the British from Canada, depriving them of the crucially important bases at Quebec and Montreal.

But the invasion of Canada, undertaken in the fall and winter of 1775, failed miserably after the invading party, suffering incredible hardships in the winter snows, had stormed Quebec on New Year's Day of 1776 and been driven off, with Arnold badly wounded and Montgomery dead. It was now the British turn to take the initiative. Holding firm to the *northern* anchor of the Hudson-Champlain line, they were certain to make a major effort to secure the *southern* end of the line.

A British design to invade New York did not mean, to be sure, that therefore they must evacuate Boston. Howe's decision here was hastened by the skill and energy with which Washington pressed the attack. Washington, having made careful plans for a full-scale invasion of Boston, began to bombard the British with captured cannon dragged across the hills all the way from Saratoga. The last straw, from Howe's point of view, came when the Yankees seized Dorchester Heights, south of Boston, on March 4, 1776, and defied the British to dislodge them. Howe did not dare make such a major assault, but he could not stay where he was with the Heights in American hands. He worked desperately amid the storm and gales of the following days to pack his equipment, embark his troops, and evacuate the town. During the night of March 14 the British sailed off. Washington, certain that an invasion of New York was imminent, moved his army there at once.

One of the soldiers who came with Washington's forces to New York in April 1776 was a twenty-four-year-old lieutenant of militia from Massachusetts, Isaac Bangs. For him, as for most small-towners then and since, visiting the big city was a real event. On April 19, scarcely more than twenty-four hours after his arrival, he spent the day sightseeing in the city, which, he wrote in his *Journal*, "I found vastly surpassing my expectations."

Bangs gazed with wonder at the old colonial fort at the very tip of Manhattan, "a very strong and costly fort, built by the King's troops and many masons for the protection of the city." Near the fort his eye was arrested by a grand and imposing statue of George III, which he described as follows:

The design was in imitation of one of the Roman Emperors on horseback. The man George is represented about ⅓ larger than a natural man; the horse, in proportion, both neatly constructed of lead gilded with gold, raised on a pedestal of white marble, about 15 feet high, enclosed with a very elegant fence about 10 feet high, the 2 lower feet stone, the remainder of open worked iron; the enclosure was oval, containing about ¼ acre of beautiful green. This, with several churches and other elegant buildings on either side of the spacious street, form a most beautiful prospect from the fort.

But, as might be expected of a soldier awaiting an attack, Bangs was interested primarily in the quite recent defenses that General Charles Lee had begun to set

*Children of a wealthy New York family,
by John Durand about 1768.*

up earlier in the year before he was called away to supervise the defense of Charleston, South Carolina. Outside the fort Bangs saw the people "busily employed" in reinforcing the old stone battery where the cannon would be stationed. Several other fortifications, he said, had been built, to make the town "tolerably strong and safe again from any attacks of the enemy." In addition, "every street leading from the water [was] almost stopped with breastworks built by General Lee on his arrival, to prevent the enemy from landing to set fire to the town."

Bangs found that New Yorkers faced a problem that could bring about their defeat in war even though their fortifications remained intact—the water supply. Water had originally been provided for the inhabitants by hand pumps sunk, in M'Roberts' words, "at convenient distances in the streets." But excessive use had brought about a crisis; the watertable had fallen so low that salt water seeping in from the harbor rendered the pump water brackish and useless for drinking purposes. Drinking water, or as the people called it, "tea water," had therefore to be brought in on carts from the pure springs in the surrounding countryside. But this was a tedious and expensive procedure; to solve the problem the City Council was engaged in the construction of a modern water-supply system.

The details of this municipal project were of absorbing interest to Isaac Bangs, and off he went to the waterworks at Brooklyn Heights to see what was going on.

The town of Brooklinn with the adjacent hills I visited, and took a full view of the waterworks that they are making to convey water through the city. . . . The work that is already done (the most difficult part) is to convey water from the side of a hill near a pond to the top of the hill, which being higher than any part of the city, the water is to be conveyed in pipes through the city.

The pipes were designed after the Roman style— hollow wooden logs, narrowed at one end and each fitted tightly into the next. A deep well had been dug, and a pump installed in it to draw the water up and to force it through the wooden pipes to an "artificial pond," or reservoir, on top of the hill.

So far so good. "All of this," Bangs wrote, "I could easily understand; but the grand question was, how was the machine in the well first actuated and continued in motion?" He was astounded to learn that this *"was wholly done by the power of boiling water."* Indeed, this was the first steam engine ever made in America, and it had been cast at the Sharp and Curtenius Iron Works in 1775. Bangs, as we may imagine, was fascinated at the sight of this wondrous, hissing, groaning, wheezing machine; it took him a long time, watching its motions and conversing in broken English and sign language with the Dutch engineer in charge, before he could figure out how it worked.

Bangs described the cylinder as "a strong copper tube of about eighteen inches in diameter and about ten feet long, which stands perpendicularly. The lower part of this tube is tight; but the upper end hath in it a movable stopper which may move upwards or downwards with as much ease as possible." This "stopper," or piston head, he said,

is kept in constant motion by the means of steam vapor; and to this stopper is fastened a stout wooden lever by a bar of iron. The lever is fastened in the middle upon an axis; and as the stopper of the tube moves upwards and downwards, it moves the lever, which worketh the engine in the well, which forceth the water into the pond at the top of the hill.

Isaac Bangs dutifully attended divine service as often as he could in one of the city's numerous churches. On May 6 he listened, at the Brick Meeting House, to an excellent sermon on the Eighth Psalm: *Thou hast put all things under man's feet: all sheep and oxen, yea, and the beasts of the field.* Though Bangs did not note the fact in his *Journal,* there were men as well as beasts underfoot in the streets of New York—there were in the city at least 5,000 black slaves, the property of well-to-do members of the community. The plight of these black people had struck M'Roberts with painful force. "It rather hurts a European eye," he said, "to see so many Negro slaves upon the streets, though they are said to diminish yearly here. . . . There are computed between 26,000 and 30,000 inhabitants; in this number are, I believe, included the slaves, who make at least a fifth part of the number."

As defensive measures went slowly forward, aided by the labor of these slaves—building fortifications, gathering arms and powder—the army watched for the British.

On June 28 there was a diversion when Thomas Hickey was hanged in a field near Bowery Lane before a vast throng of onlookers estimated at 20,000. Hickey, a member of Washington's security guard, had been drawn into a conspiracy to assassinate the commander-in-chief and, in the words of a contemporary report, to "put into execution that horrid plot of assassinating the staff officers, blowing up the magazine, and securing the passes of the town, on the arrival of the hungry ministerial myrmidons."

On June 29, the day after Hickey's execution, the "ministerial myrmidons," that is, the British forces, hove in sight. A few days later the troops were landed on Staten Island, much to the alarm of Manhattan inhabitants, many of whom made preparations for flight. The British soldiers were not too happy with their new quarters. "We sleep upon the sea shore," wrote one of them, "nothing to shelter us from the violent rains but our coats and the miserably paltry blankets." The troops suffered torments from the mosquitoes that swarmed on Staten Island, considering them "a plague greater than there can be in hell itself." But there was nothing to do about it: there they must sit and wait, while week by week Howe's forces grew larger as more ships arrived bearing Hessians from Germany and Clinton's men from South Carolina. "So vast a fleet," wrote an observer in *Freeman's Journal* when the build-up was complete, "was never before seen in the port of New York, or perhaps in all America . . . The multitude of masts carries the appearance of a wood."

The British arrived practically at the same time as

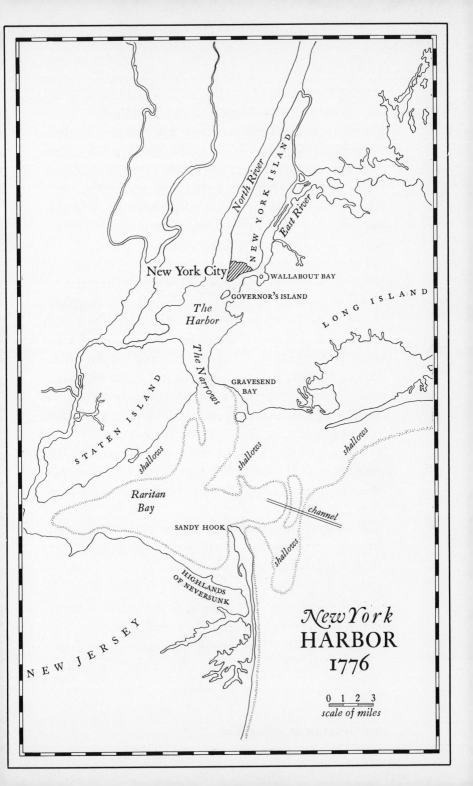

North River

NEW YORK ISLAND

East River

New York City

WALLABOUT BAY

GOVERNOR'S ISLAND

The Harbor

LONG ISLAND

The Narrows

GRAVESEND BAY

STATEN ISLAND

shallows

shallows

shallows

Raritan Bay

channel

SANDY HOOK

shallows

HIGHLANDS OF NEVERSUNK

NEW JERSEY

New York
HARBOR
1776

0 1 2 3
scale of miles

news of the signing of the Declaration of Independence. "We have the news," wrote Bangs on July 6, "of the United Colonies being declared free and independent states by the Congress." He and his fellow officers went to a tavern to celebrate, and spent the afternoon playing bowls on the bowling green—losers to pick up the wine tab. Since Bangs won, he had the additional good fortune of being able to celebrate independence without having to pay for the refreshments.

The burning oratory of the Declaration—in the very presence of British armed might—fanned the patriots' hatred of Britain to a passionate intensity. On the night of July 9, the *Pennsylvania Journal* reported, "the equestrian statue of George III, which Tory pride and folly raised in the year 1770, has by the Sons of Freedom, been laid prostrate in the dirt—the just desert of an ungrateful tyrant!" The fallen George, the practical Bangs noted with satisfaction, would be put to a good use: "The lead, we hear, is to be run up into musket balls for the use of the Yankees, when it is hoped that the emanations of the leaden George will make a deep impression on the bodies of some of his red-coated and Tory subjects."

On August 21 a frightful thunderstorm hit the city; the judgment of God, evidently, was at hand. The *Pennsylvania Journal* testified that it was

One of the most dreadful we ever witnessed; it lasted from 7 til 10 o'clock. Several claps [bolts] struck in and about New York. Many houses were damaged and several lives lost. Three officers, a captain and two lieuten-

FOR EXPORTATION. FIFTY
POUNDS PENALTY IF RELAN-
DED, AND TWENTY POUNDS
IF SOLD OR USED IN GREAT
BRITAIN.

*King, Queen, and wrapper from a deck of
English playing cards imported in 1765.*

ants, belonging to Col. McDougall's regiment, were struck instantly dead. The points of their swords, for several inches, were melted, with a few silver dollars they had in their pockets . . . A dog in the same tent was also killed, and a soldier near it struck blind, deaf, and dumb. One in the main street was killed, as likewise ten on Long Island. Two or three were much burnt, and greatly hurt. When God speaks, who can but fear?

Next day, the British struck. Thousands of men poured ashore at Gravesend Bay on Long Island, stormed through the wooded hills that lay between them and the main American encampment at Brooklyn village, fell upon the defenders and put them to flight. With the British fleet patrolling the East River in their rear, it looked as though nothing could keep the American forces from destruction or capture. But Washington saved the situation by evacuating his men in open boats, under the very noses of the British, through the night of August 29. Howe, in a letter to Lord Germain, estimated the American losses at 3,300 in killed and drowned, prisoners and wounded. The actual figure was perhaps half of Howe's estimate; most of these were prisoners.

When Washington finally reunited his forces he may have had 16,000 to Howe's 21,000. Then the British struck again, this time invading Manhattan, on September 15. At about ten in the morning, wrote the *Freeman's Journal*, the British troops, "under cover of a tremendous fire from eight or ten ships of war, effected a landing near Mr. Stuyvesant's house in the Bowery, and in a few hours took possession of New York."

The Americans streamed northward up the island, in retreat before the British. Lieutenant Mackenzie, whom we last met at Lexington, crossed over from Long Island to Manhattan with the invading force. "The rebels," he reported contemptuously, "left a great quantity of cannon, ammunition, stores, provisions, tents, etc., behind them, and abandoned those immense works which had cost them infinite labor and pains, without making the least attempt to defend one of them."

But on September 16 the British received a disagreeable surprise. At Morningside Heights, sheep and cattle grazed over the rocky pastures where Columbia University now stands. There the very same militia that had run in panic from the British the day before, turned upon their pursuers; they stubbornly held their ground in an engagement involving 5,000 men on each side. The indecisive battle gave rise to one of the most famous songs of the Revolution. It tells of a British grenadier who was mortally wounded during the action, and died the following day in the hands of his captors. Dying, he tells his story: *I left England in 1774, saw action in Boston, came to New York with Howe. They told us we'd have an easy time with these Yankees. Not so. Wherever we have trod, men have sprung up like grasshoppers. They die so easily, so gladly, for freedom!*

American plough, about 1740.

The Dying Redcoat

(Guitar Instrumental)

Voice

'Twas on De - cem - ber's fif - teenth day, When we set_ sail_ for A - mer - i - ca; 'Twas

drums do beat and trum-pets sound, And un - to ___ Bos - ton ___ we ___ were bound.

And when to Boston we did come,
We thought by the aid of our British guns
To drive the rebels from that place
And fill their hearts with sore disgrace.
But to our sad and sore surprise,
We saw men like grasshoppers rise:
They fought like heroes much enraged
Which surely frightened General Gage.

Like lions roaring for their prey,
They feared no danger nor dismay;
True British blood runs through their veins
And them with courage yet sustains.
We saw those bold Columbia sons,
Spread death and slaughter from their guns,
Freedom or death! was all their cry,
They did not seem to fear to die.

146 *Trumpet of a Prophecy*

We sailed to York, as you've been told,
With the loss of many a Briton bold,
For to make those rebels own our King,
And daily tribute to him bring.
They said it was a garden place,
And that our armies could, with ease,
Pull down their towns, lay waste their lands,
In spite of all their boasted bands.

A garden place it was indeed,
And in it grew many a bitter weed,
Which did pull down our highest hopes
And sorely wound the British troops.
'Tis now September the seventeenth day,
I wish I'd ne'er come to America,
Full fifteen hundred have been slain
Bold British heroes every one.

Now I've received my deathly wound,
I bid farewell to England's ground;
My wife and children will mourn for me,
Whilst I lie cold in America.
Fight on, America's noble sons,
Fear not Britannia's thundering guns,
Maintain your rights from year to year,
God's on your side, you need not fear.

When, a few days later, a disastrous fire broke out in the city, it was natural for the British command to conclude that the Americans were now attempting to rob them by treachery of the fruits of victory that they had been unable to take in the open field.

The fire, reported the *New York Gazette* on September 30, "broke out at the most southerly part of the city, near Whitehall, and was discovered between 12 and 1 o'clock in the morning, the wind blowing very fresh from the south, and the weather exceeding dry." Some 600 houses were demolished before the holocaust was over. Among the beautiful buildings that perished was Trinity Church, whose exquisite steeple had been completed only in 1772. The *Gazette* continued:

Long before the main fire reached Trinity Church, that large, ancient, and venerable edifice was in flames, which baffled every effort to suppress them. The steeple, which was one hundred and forty feet high, the upper part wood . . . resembled a vast pyramid of fire, exhibiting a most grand and awful spectacle. Several women and children perished in the fire. Their shrieks, joined to the roaring of the flames, the crush of falling houses, and the widespread ruin which everywhere appeared, formed a scene of horror beyond description.

Numbers were made homeless. "The sick, the aged, women and children," wrote Mackenzie, "were seen going they knew not where, and taking refuge in houses which were at a distance from the fire, but from whence they were in several instances driven a second and even a third time by the devouring element, and at last in a state of despair laying themselves down on the Common."

As the fire burned itself out, Washington was encamped on Harlem Heights, near the northern end of Manhattan. He was enraged because the militia, whom he called "arrant cowards," were leaving the army by the hundreds, even thousands.

Putting out a fire,
as depicted on a New York firemen's
certificate of the period.

Though there may have been cowards among the militia, all the militia were not cowards; their flight had nothing personal about it. It's all very well (they might have said) for you, general, to swear at us; but it's too late in the year to be fighting; we've got to get the crops in. You, general, are a wealthy man; there's no fear that *your* crops will rot in the fields if you don't go home— your black slaves will bring them in. But we are poor people, and we have no slaves. If we don't bring our own crops in, our wives will have to leave the children, and go into the fields; or, worse still, they won't be harvested at all. And then where will we be? Manhattan Island, what's more, is surrounded by water and the British fleet; it's no place to be when the British army is after you.

On September 21, from a platform provided through the courtesy of General Howe, a militiaman spoke to the soldiers, and to the nation, on the meaning of war and man's life. The platform was a scaffold. Mackenzie recorded in his *Diary* that Nathan Hale,

a lieutenant in the rebel army and a native of Connecti-cut, was apprehended as a spy, last night on Long Island; and having this day made full and free confession to the Commander-in-Chief of his being employed by Mr. Washington in this capacity, he was hanged at 11 o'clock in front of the park of artillery. He was about 24 years of age, and had been educated at the college of New Haven [Yale] in Connecticut. He behaved with great composure and resolution, saying he thought it the duty of every good officer to obey any orders given him by his com-mander-in-chief; and desired the spectators to be at all times prepared to meet death in whatever shape it might appear.

Nathan Hale was a schoolmaster by trade. His words, whispered at the rim of eternity, spoke to unawakened hearts as the trumpet of a prophecy. With the halter around his neck he addressed the populace. *"The British,"* the *Freeman's Journal* reported him as saying, *"are shedding the blood of the innocent. If I had ten thousand lives, I would lay them all down in defense of this injured, bleeding country."*

*George Washington
on horseback, from a
Pennsylvania Dutch pie plate.*

Ballad of Nathan Hale

Ami.   C   E

Hale   in   the   bush;   For   Hale   in   the   bush.

Cooling shades of the night were coming apace,
    The tattoo had beat; the tattoo had beat.
The noble one sprang from his dark lurking place,
    To make his retreat; to make his retreat.

He warily trod on the dry rustling leaves,
    As he pass'd through the wood; as he pass'd through the
    wood;
And silently gained his rude launch on the shore,
    As she played with the flood; as she played with the flood.

The guards of the camp, on that dark, dreary night,
    Had a murderous will; had a murderous will.
They took him and bore him afar from the shore,
    To a hut on the hill; to a hut on the hill.

They took him and bound him and bore him away,
    Down the hill's grassy side; down the hill's grassy side;
'Twas there the base hirelings in royal array,
    His cause did deride; his cause did deride.

The faith of a martyr, the tragedy showed,
    As he trod the last stage; as he trod the last stage.
And Briton's will shudder at gallant Hale's blood,
    As his words do presage; as his words do presage.

Throughout October Washington withdrew his forces from Manhattan across King's Bridge at the island's northern tip, and concentrated his men at White Plains, in Westchester County. Here Howe caught up with him, and joined battle on October 28. "The scene was grand and solemn," wrote an American officer, "all the adjacent hills smoked as though on fire, and bellowed and trembled with a perpetual cannonade." The Americans continued to withdraw, and Howe paused to reduce Fort Washington, which commanded the Manhattan approach to King's Bridge. He took the fortress with ease on November 17, and with it some 2,500 American prisoners. Lieutenant Mackenzie inspected these men after the surrender. "The rebel prisoners," he recorded, "were in general but very indifferently clothed; few of them appeared to have a second shirt, nor did they appear to have washed themselves during the campaign. A great many of them were lads under 15, and old men; and few of them had the appearance of soldiers. Their odd figures frequently excited the laughter of our soldiers."

A few days later a British detachment under Lord Cornwallis crossed the Hudson to take Fort Lee, rout Washington's troops, and occupy New Jersey. As Washington retreated southward before the British, his army melted away around him. Reaching the Delaware early in December, he set to work frantically scrounging boats to take his men across: the last of his men rowed over to the Pennsylvania side minutes before Cornwallis arrived. Washington was seized with a black despair. With only a couple of thousand men, how could he hope to prevail against the mightiest empire in the world? "The game is nearly up," wrote the commander-in-chief on December 20. "Ten more days will put an end to the existence of our army."

Yes, it was clear that the Revolution was dying. On this score Billy Howe was, by the middle of December 1776, quite in agreement with Washington. Howe settled himself comfortably in winter quarters in New York. There would be time enough in the spring to mop up the scattered rebel bands in Pennsylvania. The main task in 1777 would be to occupy the Hudson Valley and finish off the New Englanders. With this in mind Howe ordered an expedition to sail for Rhode Island. The troop transports weighed anchor on December 1, passed through Hell's Gate with a fine following wind, and landed on Rhode Island on December 8. There was no opposition from the Yankees, but the men passed a rough first night. "As the troops could not get their tents ashore from the transports," wrote Lieutenant Mackenzie, "they were obliged to lie without any shelter, on a bleak hill, much exposed to the severity of the weather." Others, who advanced up the island chasing the rebel militia, were fortunate enough to get shelter in barns and houses.

If, therefore, Howe lost Boston in 1776, he won Newport the same year. And a very good base it was, too, from which to invade New England: tit for tat!

As we now know, both Washington's gloom and Howe's optimism were misplaced. What actually *did* make it possible for the Revolution to survive the crisis of 1776?

One factor was the education with respect to the facts of life that British occupation brought to the people of New Jersey. Any illusions that they might have had about the "kindly" British were roughly dispelled by the actual shock of war and invasion. A *Brief Narrative of the Ravages of the British and Hessians*, written by an unknown author in the spring of 1777, details the sufferings that the inhabitants of the Princeton area underwent when the British and the Hessians arrived in December 1776. The experiences recounted here were duplicated in many other communities. The invaders, says our author,

> not only burnt up all the firewood that the inhabitants had provided for winter, but stripped shops, outhouses and some dwelling houses of the boards that covered them, and all the loose boards and timber that the joiners and carpenters had in store to work up; they burnt, with all, their fences and garden inclosures within the town, and afterwards sent their carriages and drew away the farmers' fences adjoining within a mile, and laid all in common. They also cut down apple trees and other fruit-bearing trees and burnt them . . .

British and Hessians made wholesale raids upon the outlying farms, stole slaves, stole horses, killed cattle and sheep. They made themselves at home in the farmers' houses, occupied their best bedrooms, stole their corn and fodder to feed their mounts. "At a gentleman farmer's house the next to where I now live," the *Narrative*'s author charged, there was, with officers and all, one hundred and seventy of those genteel unwelcome guests. His best rooms and beds in his house were taken up by the officers, who were fed upon the best diet that the house afforded. The soldiers took and wasted what they pleased of his stalk tops and oats in the sheaf in making sheds to keep them from the cold when they stood on guard, besides what their horses devoured.

These depredations were endless, and they were accompanied by insult, mockery, and abuse. "To give a particular account," lamented the *Narrative*, "of every robbery and outrage committed by the Hessians and Regulars in and within five miles of Princeton would fill a volume."

As the temper of the people changed in the face of these outrages, George Washington gave concrete proof that a military force was still in existence to challenge British tyranny and to rally mass support. In the days before Christmas, happy Hessians in the Trenton and Princeton garrisons were trimming their Christmas trees; but the patriots, by their campfires, were listening to the reading of a paper. It had been written by Tom Paine, marching with them across New Jersey. "These are the times that try men's souls," it said. "The summer soldier and the sunshine patriot will, in this crisis, shrink from the service of his country; but he that stands it now, deserves the love and thanks of man and woman."

Fortified by these singing words, the revolutionary army crossed the Delaware early on Christmas Day in the midst of an icy, howling blizzard and attacked the

Hessian garrison at Trenton. "The American army," said the *Freeman's Journal*,

which did not exceed 2,400 men, crossed the Delaware with several companies of artillery, and 13 field-pieces, and formed in two divisions; one commanded by General Greene, the other by General Sullivan, and the whole by General Washington. . . . The impetuosity of our men was irresistible; fifteen minutes decided the action, and the enemy threw down their arms and surrendered [as] prisoners of war. . . . The army returned the same day, and, notwithstanding a continual pelting for twelve hours, of a most violent rain, hail and snow storm, we had only two men frozen to death.

Soon the British were obliged to pull in their southern New Jersey garrisons and withdraw in the direction of New York. As the occupiers moved out, Washington's forces moved in. "The rebels," wrote one of Howe's officers, "were scattered about the country, and took up their quarters in the different towns the troops had withdrawn from. They were frequently very troublesome to us, and every foraging party that went out, was pretty certain to have a skirmish with them."

The presence of the Continental forces, we may imagine, greatly inspired the local militia. "They made a practice," wrote the same British officer, "of waylaying single persons, or very small bodies [of men] on the roads, and killing them from behind trees or other cover, in a most savagelike manner. . . . When we showed up in any force they disappeared till we returned to our quarters."

Even after the British had withdrawn completely from the state in June 1777, the Jerseyites continued to keep careful watch for British marauders from Staten Island or New York. General William Winds, a New Jersey militia general, issued these instructions to his town commanders in September 1777:

You are to keep one man always with an order already written to impress any horse on the way that he shall want. Upon the first appearance of the enemy's coming to attack you or yours, you are to dispatch the man and tell him to come the nighest road to me or my house; and he is to call to every man, woman, and child he sees, and desire them to call upon all men to push down to where the enemy is and give them battle. But he is not to stop to tell his story, but call out as he rides along. . . . If they have no guns or ammunition they are to carry pitchforks, flails, stones or such weapons as they choose or think best. But if any man is afraid to go to battle that hath no gun, he is immediately to set out as a common crier towards the back country and desire everyone he sees to come down to the help of the Lord against the mighty.

Two years after Lexington there would be a Paul Revere in every community; David would go against Goliath, armed with stones.

THE NETHER MILLSTONE

Prisoners of War, 1775–1780

His heart is as firm as a stone;
Yea, firm as the nether millstone.

Book of Job

When the British took New York they also took, for the first time in the war, many thousands of American prisoners, some in the campaign on Long Island, some as the result of the surrender of Fort Washington. Until the end of the war New York City and its harbor remained a main center for the detention of American prisoners of war. What kind of treatment did the ordinary soldier or sailor receive at the hands of the British and their Tory allies?

From November 1776 to May 1777 an American officer, Colonel Ethan Allen, was on parole in the city, that is, he was a prisoner of war who had been granted his liberty on his solemn promise, as an officer and a gentleman, that he would not run away and rejoin the American forces. During this time Allen was free to observe and record the treatment of American soldiers in

British hands. The narrative that he published later is an interesting and on the whole truthful picture of the lot of American prisoners of war; it casts much light upon prison conditions in New York in particular.

Allen was the leader of the Green Mountain Boys, and he had made history in 1775 by capturing Fort Ticonderoga. He and a number of his comrades were made prisoners later that year when they attempted, during the invasion of Canada, to capture Montreal in the same bold fashion. They were put in irons and shipped off to England.

Allen related that he and his men—a band of about thirty soldiers—were captured in October 1775 and placed on board a British ship, the H.M.S. *Gaspee*, off Montreal in the Gulf of St. Lawrence. Allen was loaded with irons, "so close upon my ankles, that I could not lie down in any other manner than on my back," and thrust down "into the lowest and most wretched part of the vessel, where I got the favor of a chest to sit on, the same answered for my bed at night." Allen's predicament was painful in the extreme, but he singled out a number of his captors for praise, because they were humane people and showed him kindness; one officer of the *Gaspee*, by the name of Bradley, "was very generous to me, he would often send me victuals from his own table; nor did a day fail, but that he sent me a good drink of grog."

Early in November 1775, Allen and his comrades were transferred to H.M.S. *Adamant* bound for England, and here their sufferings began in earnest. Also on board was a group of American Tories, including Colonel Guy

Johnson, who, said Allen, inflamed the feelings of the captain and crew against the prisoners; and they were thrust down into a narrow, stifling compartment below decks. "Rather than die," he said,

I submitted to their indignities, being drove with bayonnets into the filthy dungeon, with the other prisoners, where we were denied fresh water, except a small allowance, which was very inadequate to our wants; and in consequence of the stench of the place, each of us was soon followed with a diarrhoea and fever, which occasioned intolerable thirst. When we asked for water, we were most commonly (instead of obtaining it) insulted and derided; and to add to all the horrors of the place, it was so dark that we could not see each other, and were overspread with body lice.

The prisoners lived in this state for nearly six weeks, until the *Adamant* reached England in December 1775. Allen steeled himself to face the fact that he was in the power of "a haughty and cruel nation" that would treat him as a rebel rather than a prisoner of war, and would hang him. But to his surprise he and his friends were shut up in Pendennis Castle, near Falmouth, and kindly treated. The jailer, Lieutenant Hamilton, sent the colonel every day "a fine breakfast and dinner from his own table, and a bottle of good wine." The men were housed together in a clean room, given straw to sleep on, and were able to rid themselves of lice.

Early in 1776 the British government made the decision that it would not hang Allen and his comrades but would return them to America to exchange for equal-ranking British prisoners taken by the Americans. Allen and his party made the trip with the troop convoy that brought forces for Sir Peter Parker and Sir Henry Clinton's invasion of South Carolina. The prisoners were placed aboard H.M.S. *Solebay*, twenty-eight guns, which was to take part in the bombardment of Fort Moultrie. Allen recorded that the captain of the *Solebay* was extremely rude and unpleasant, but that the prisoners received kind and hospitable treatment from some of the officers and men. Allen himself shared a bunk with the master of arms, Callaghan, and lived on the friendliest terms with him until the end of the journey; and the *Solebay*'s surgeon took good care of those who became sick. Sickness was no minor hazard. Many men were carried off by scurvy, which was due to inadequate diet, and many soldiers on the troop transports lost their lives from the smallpox infection that raged among them.

It is amusing to record that when the convoy put in at the Irish port of Cork in January 1776 the local people staged a demonstration of affection for Allen and his men, sending on board many gifts for

the relief and support of the prisoners, who were thirty-four in number, and in very needy circumstances. A suit of clothes from head to foot, including an overcoat, or surtout, with two shirts, were bestowed on each of them. My suit I received in super-fine broadcloth, sufficient for two jackets, . . . eight fine Holland shirts and stocks ready made, with a number of pairs of silk and worsted hose, two pair of shoes, two beaver hats. . . . *The Irish gentlemen furthermore made a large gratuity of wines of the best sort, old spirits, Geneva, loaf and brown sugar, coffee, tea and chocolate, with a large round of pickled beef, and a number of fat turkies.*

Captain Symonds of the *Solebay* was furious when he found out, and confiscated most of the good things, swearing that "the damned American rebels should not be feasted at this date by the damned rebels of Ireland." The reason for Irish warmth toward the Americans was that they had been living and suffering under British rule for centuries, and had made many bloody and unsuccessful uprisings against their oppressors. Understandably they had great admiration for the American militiamen who fought at Lexington, Concord, and Bunker Hill, and as good Catholics they offered their fervent prayers for the success of the American Revolution.

The fleet left Cork about February 12, 1776, and, much delayed by storms, arrived off Cape Fear, North Carolina, early in May. The prisoners were transferred to H.M.S. *Mercury* and sent to Halifax, where, after suffering severely from hunger and scurvy, they were placed aboard a man o' war bound for New York. Captain Smith welcomed Allen with kindness and assured him that he and his men would be treated, as befitted soldiers and honorable men, with decency and respect. "This was so unexpected, and so sudden a transition," Allen wrote, "that it drew tears from my eyes, which all the ill usage I had before met with, was not able to produce."

The ship arrived in New York in October 1776, and Allen was paroled in November along with his fellow officers. As for the other prisoners, they "were put into the filthy churches in New York, with the distressed prisoners that were taken at Fort Washington." Allen was restricted to New York, but free to walk the streets and observe the behavior of the British and their Tory allies toward the defeated foe.

According to the estimate of the British themselves, there were at this time 3,000 American prisoners of war in the city. Lieutenant Mackenzie noted in his diary on November 5 that American soldiers were wretchedly clad and that "the Rebel Army must suffer greatly as soon as the severe weather sets in. It is a fact that many of the Rebels who were killed in the late affairs, were without shoes or stockings, and several were observed to have only linen drawers on, with a rifle or hunting shirt, without any proper shirt or waistcoat. They are also in great want of blankets."

The plight of the prisoners excited widespread anger and distress among the patriots, but not everyone believed that the nakedness of the soldiers was entirely their own fault. "As soon as they were taken," a correspondent wrote to the *Freeman's Journal*, on January 19, 1777,

they were robbed of all their baggage, of whatever money they had, though it were of paper, and could be of no advantage to the enemy, of their silver shoe-buckles, and knee-buckles, etc., and many were stripped almost naked of their clothes. Especially those who had good clothes, were stripped at once, being told that such clothes were too good for rebels. Thus deprived of their clothes and baggage they were unable to shift even their linen, and were obliged to wear the same shirts for even three or four months together.

The prisoners were first placed on ships in the harbor, then transferred to churches throughout the city. On November 12 Colonel Miles, senior officer among the prisoners, wrote to General Washington and complained bitterly of disease, mortality, and hunger among these naked men, and urged the commander-in-chief to make immediate efforts for an exchange. But Lieutenant Mackenzie discounted these complaints:

With respect to their provisions, they have no real cause of complaint, as they are served with the same kind of provisions issued to the King's troops, at two-third allowance, which is the same as given to the King's troops when on board transports. They certainly are very sickly, owing to their want of clothing and necessaries, salt provisions, confinement, foul air, and little exercise. They are confined principally in the churches, sugar houses, and other large buildings, and have the liberty of walking in the yards. But they are such low-spirited creatures . . . that if once they are taken sick they seldom recover.

The patriots did not think that the blame for the situation could be shifted so easily to the prisoners themselves. "When winter came on," wrote the correspondent of the *Freeman's Journal*, our people suffered severely for want of fire and clothes to keep them warm. They were confined to churches where there were no fireplaces, that they could not make fires even if they had wood. But wood was allowed them only for cooking their pittance of victuals; and for that purpose very sparingly. They had none to keep them warm even in the extremest of weather, although they were almost naked, and the few clothes that were left upon them were their summer clothes. Nor had they a single blanket or any bedding, not even straw, allowed them til a little before Christmas.

This scene of hundreds of filthy, naked, shivering men herded together amid their excrement on the bare boards and pavements of stinking barns and churches was confirmed by Allen:

The private soldiers were crowded into churches, and environed with slavish Hessian guards . . . by merciless Britons . . . but above all by the hellish delight and triumph of the Tories over them, as they were dying by the hundreds. This was too much for me to bear as a spectator, for I saw the Tories exulting over the dead bodies of their countrymen murdered. I have gone into the churches and seen sundry of the prisoners in the agonies of death, in consequence of very hunger, and others speechless and near death, biting pieces of chips; others pleading, for God's sake, for something to eat, and at the same time shivering with the cold.

The corpses were dragged out of these charnel houses

and, in Allen's expressive phrase, "slightly buried." The *Freeman's Journal* tells us in more detail:

They dragged them out of their prisons by one leg or one arm, piled them up out of doors, there let them lie till a sufficient number were dead to make a cart load; then loaded them up in a cart, drove the cart thus loaded out to the ditches made by our people when fortifying New York; there they would tip the cart, tumble the corpses together into the ditch, and afterwards slightly cover them with earth.

The *Journal* estimated that the number of men who died in the New York prisons as a result of this treatment was "1,500 brave Americans, who had nobly gone forth in defense of their injured, oppressed country, but whom the chance of war had cast into the hands of our enemies."

When the corpses were carried off, Allen noted, "whole gangs of Tories would laugh and say 'there goes another load of damned rebels.' " He made at this point an important observation about the use of the word "rebel." Any brutality, any cruelty might be inflicted on a man if he was a "rebel." The label was enough to sanctify the practice of unmentionable atrocities upon otherwise innocent human beings and to discharge the tormentor from any obligation to show charity, compassion, or elementary human decency toward a captured foe. "The word 'rebel,' " Allen wrote, "applied to any vanquished persons, without regard to rank . . . was thought by the enemy sufficient to sanctify whatever cruelties they were pleased to inflict, death itself not excepted."

What of Mackenzie's charge that Americans were "low-spirited creatures" who lacked the will and the manhood to survive disease and difficulty? The British used hunger and the fear of death as a *weapon* with which to press prisoners into His Majesty's service. One young man, reduced to a living skeleton, informed Colonel Allen "that he and his brother had been urged to enlist in the British service, but that both had resolved to die first; that his brother had died last night . . . and that he expected shortly to follow him." Allen advised the youth to enlist and then desert, but the young soldier was troubled by the question, Was such a thing right in the sight of God? Allen commented that the integrity shown by these common soldiers, their dedication to their country and its honorable cause, was "hardly credible." He believed that hundreds of men had preferred death to enlistment in the British service.

The Americans who survived these cruelties acquired exchange value after Washington's victories at Trenton and Princeton in January 1777 provided Hessian prisoners for whom they could be exchanged. They were, accordingly, set free; but many died of exhaustion on their way to the American lines; others lived out miserable lives as invalids, too broken in health ever to be fully restored. "Their constitutions are broken," lamented the *Freeman's Journal*, "the stamina of nature worn out, they cannot recover—they die."

If the lot of soldiers captured in the struggle was often bad, that of American sailors made prisoner on the high seas was infinitely worse. Thousands of American seamen languished and died on prison hulks in New York Harbor until the end of the war.

The most notorious of these ships was the *Jersey*, an obsolete and rotting man o' war anchored at Wallabout Bay, on the Long Island shore, into which seamen were dumped for the duration of their captivity. These men had composed the crews of privateers, or armed merchantmen, which sailed mainly from New England ports to harass British commerce and capture British ships. Many of the privateers were themselves captured by the British navy and taken to New York.

A number of accounts survive that testify to the sufferings undergone by prisoners on board the *Jersey*, all of whom were captured seamen. One of the most vivid records was composed by Captain Thomas Dring, and published in 1829. Captain Dring sailed as mate on a privateer called the *Chance* from Providence, Rhode Island, in 1782. The ship was soon captured by the British man o' war *Belisarius*; the forty-man crew was put in irons, returned to New York, and thrust into the *Jersey*. Here, during a five-month captivity, Dring witnessed "the unspeakable sufferings of that wretched class of American prisoners [i.e., seamen] who were there taught the utmost extent of human misery."

The prisoners of the *Jersey* were housed on the middle and lower decks—black dungeons lighted and ventilated only by tiny portholes along the sides of the ship. Here they lived amid a stench beyond description, and in "a stifled and suffocating heat." Even here, there were levels of suffering. Officers were assigned to the gun room at the rear of the middle deck, on which native-born American seamen were housed. Foreign-born men were on the deck below, which, Dring says,

was inhabited by the most wretched in appearance of our miserable company. From the disgusting and squalid appearance of the groups which I saw ascending the stairs . . . it must have been more dismal, if possible, than that part of the hulk where I resided. . . . The faces of many of them were covered with dirt and filth; their long hair and beards [were] matted and foul: [they were] clothed in rags, and with scarcely a sufficient supply of these to cover their disgusting bodies. Many among them possessed no clothing except the remnants of those garments which they wore when first brought aboard.

The prisoners were divided into "messes" of six men. Each mess was issued two-thirds of the daily food allowance given by the navy to an equivalent number of able-bodied British seamen—biscuit, pork, oatmeal, dried peas, and beef, but no fresh vegetables or fruit of any kind. The food was of indifferent quality; the bread, scanty as it was, moldy and filled with worms. Each mess prepared its food on a boiler, or "great copper," which was housed in the forward part of the middle deck. As soon as one prisoner completed the cooking for his messmates, "another supplicant stood ready to take his place; and thus they continued to throng the galley, during the whole time that the fire was allowed to remain under the great copper."

Years later Captain Dring still retained a vivid memory of "those emaciated beings, moving from the galley, with their wretched pittance of meat; each creeping to the spot where his messmates were assembled, to divide it with a group of haggard and sickly creatures, their garments hanging in tatters round their meager limbs, and the hue of death upon their careworn faces." We may well believe, as Dring assures us, that the prisoners rose from their meal "in torments from the cravings of unsatisfied hunger and thirst."

The ship's crew in charge of the *Jersey* was very small, less than seventeen officers and men. A military guard was set over the prisoners "composed of soldiers from the different regiments quartered on Long Island. The number usually on duty on board was about thirty. Each week they were relieved by a fresh party." The guard had little to do with the prisoners unless they attempted to escape, and left them alone for the most part. The prisoners established their own regulations governing conduct and carried out their own punishments. These rules, Dring tells us,

were chiefly directed to the preservation of personal cleanliness, and the prevention of immorality. For a refusal to comply with any one of them, the refractory prisoner was subject to a stated punishment. It is an astonishing fact that any rules thus made should have so long existed and been enforced among a multitude of men situated as we were. . . . Among our rules were the following: that personal cleanliness should be preserved, as far as was practicable; that profane language should be avoided; that *theft should be severely punished; and that no smoking should be permitted between decks, by day or night, on account of the annoyance which it caused to the sick.*

Essential work on board the *Jersey* was done by the able-bodied men taken in rotation. The group chosen for a given day was called "a working party," and each member received, as a reward for his services, "a full allowance of provisions, and a half-pint of rum each per day; with the privilege of going on deck early in the morning, to breathe the pure air." The pure air alone, Dring contended, without the rum or extra food, was "a sufficient compensation for all the duty which was required."

The working parties washed down the deck and gangways, hoisted up wood, water, and supplies from the tenders, emptied the latrine tubs, took care of the sick, and brought up the dead. On fine days the prisoners might come to the upper deck and stay there till sunset, content "to breathe the cool air of the approaching night, and [feel] the luxury of our evening pipe." But the period of respite was brief. When the sun fell the swarms of prisoners had to descend again to their black dungeons, to the terrifying night where

silence was a stranger to our dark abode. The groans of the sick and dying; the curses poured out by weary and exhausted men upon our inhuman keepers; the restlessness caused by the suffocating heat and the confined and poisonous air; mingled with the wild and incoherent ravings of delirium, were the sounds, which every night were raised around us.

"Prisoners Starving to Death,"
by John Trumbull.

On the upper deck the sentinels were stationed, wheeling and pacing through the night with challenge, counter-challenge, and the ringing cry, "All's well!"

The prisoners on the *Jersey* made careful preparations to observe Independence Day. Dring tells us:

A few days before July the fourth, we made such preparations as our circumstances would admit for an observance of the anniversary of American independence. We had procured some supplies wherewith to make ourselves merry on the occasion; and intended to spend the day in such innocent pastime and amusement as our situation would afford. . . . We thought that, although prisoners, we had a right, on that day at least, to sing and be merry. As soon as we were permitted to go on deck in the morning, thirteen little national flags were displayed in a row upon the booms. We were soon ordered by the guard to take them away; and as we neglected to obey the command, they triumphantly demolished and trampled them underfoot.

Men who became seriously ill were not taken care of by the working parties, but were sent to neighboring hospital ships anchored in Wallabout Bay. Corpses were sent ashore for burial, and prisoners eagerly volunteered to accompany them. Dring went ashore with one of these groups when Robert Carver, a gunner on the *Chance*, became sick and died. The party landed, placed the corpses on wheelbarrows, dug a trench in the sand, and buried the dead with no ceremony—no clergy were allowed to visit the *Jersey*, divine service was not performed, many of the dead were buried naked, without even a blanket to shroud them. The guards hustled the burial party through the operation, which "appeared to produce no more effect upon [them], than if we were burying dead animals instead of men." As Dring marched back to the shore, he saw "parts of many bodies which were exposed to view, although they had probably been placed there, with the same mockery of interment, but a few days before."

As the men went along, "it was a high gratification for us to bury our feet in the sand, and to shove them through it, as we passed on our way. We went by a small patch of turf, some pieces of which we tore up from the earth, and obtained permission to carry them on board, for our comrades to smell them." When the party went aboard the *Jersey*, the prisoners snatched Dring's piece of turf from him, "every fragment being passed from hand to hand, and its smell inhaled, as if it had been a fragrant rose."

Thus white Americans, fighting for independence, came to feel the same agonies that black slaves endured when torn from their African earth, to sicken and die on the slaving ships.

Months of this kind of deprivation produced deep changes. The prisoners' hearts withered with their bodies; they lost man's natural love for man, cheated each other, stole each other's pitiable possessions, and fought savagely for necessities like water. "It is impossible," wrote Dring, "to describe the struggle that ensued in consequence of our haste and exertions to procure a draught" when fresh water was brought on board. "Their feelings had become withered, and self-preservation appeared to be their only wish."

But this did not mean that the prisoners, with all their sufferings, were ready to accept life on British terms. Dring confirmed of the seamen what Ethan Allen had noted of American soldiers in New York City, that they preferred death to impressment.

A regiment of Refugees [Tories] with a green uniform was then quartered at Brooklyn. We were invited to join this Royal Band, and to partake of his Majesty's pardon and bounty. But the prisoners . . . spurned this insulting offer. They preferred to linger and die, rather than desert their country's cause. During the whole period of my confinement, I never knew a single instance of enlistment from among the prisoners of the Jersey.

After five months on the *Jersey*, Captain Dring and his fellows from the *Chance* had the good fortune to be exchanged as a result of an American capture of English seamen, who were brought to New York by a cartel, or prisoner-exchange ship. As the cartel sailed back to Providence bearing the crew of the *Chance*, Captain Dring stood upon the sloop's deck, gazed upon the night sky for the first time since his captivity, and looked with wonder on a million bright and steadfast stars.

THE CANNON AND THE DRUMS
Saratoga, 1777

O'er Champlain, proud Burgoyne all terrible comes,
With thundering cannon, and drums, and drums.

"The Capture of Burgoyne"

By April 1777 the war had run for two years. Wherever the British had sought a foothold on the continent they had been repulsed. After two years' expenditure of blood and effort all that the invaders had to show for their pains was a handful of islands, principally Rhode Island in New England, Staten and Manhattan islands in New York. They had been driven from Boston, from New Jersey, from North and South Carolina. But the government in London paid little heed to these reverses, and did not ponder their meaning; they cherished a contempt for colonial rebels. That the American people would fight and die on the cold ground, that they would grow gaunt with hunger, that they would march to war barefoot and half naked, this the British lords did not believe and could not understand. In this people they saw only a rabble of left-footed bumpkins who with a show of force could be brought back speedily to their old-time allegiance.

Spring 1777: a new year, a new campaign. Lord George Germain, Secretary of State for the Colonies, was still confident that the war could be won in a single campaign. It seemed to him a sensible idea to continue the offensive of the previous year, and to build upon the advantages won in 1776: that is, with secure bases in Montreal and New York City, to drive for the conquest and occupation of the Hudson Valley and Lake Champlain. The invasion forces would make a junction at Albany; New England would be sealed off from the rest of the mainland colonies. The conquest of the rebellion could then be undertaken piecemeal.

In February 1777 Lord Germain gave the command of the invasion forces that would move down from Canada to "Gentleman Johnny" Burgoyne, and at the same time approved General Howe's campaign plans for the new year. Howe, strange to say, considered that, with the forces available to him, the best thing he could do was to attack and occupy Philadelphia. Germain, in other words, approved two directly contradictory battle plans at the same time. Many people have found this puzzling, and as yet no very good explanation has been given—except perhaps the rambling incompetence of Britain's Secretary of State.

Burgoyne left England in March and reached Canada in May 1777. There he placed himself at the head of a fine army of British and German regulars numbering 10,000. The troops were embarked at Cumberland Head, on Lake Champlain, in June and sailed in a long string of transports up the blue waters to the fortress at Crown Point. Here, poised for the attack on his first objective, Ticonderoga, Gentleman Johnny took up his pen and wrote a declaration to the American nation. Gentleman Johnny first of all introduced himself with a pompous flourish:

By John Burgoyne Esquire, Lieutenant-General of His Majesty's armies in America, Colonel of the Queen's regiment of light dragoons, Governor of Fort William, in North Britain, one of the Representatives of the Commons of Great Britain in Parliament, and commanding an army and fleet on an expedition from Canada, etc., etc., etc.

Yes, General John Burgoyne was certainly a very important gentleman. But modesty dictated that he should not list *all* his grand offices and imposing titles. This was the meaning of the three "et ceteras."

After these flourishes Gentleman Johnny got down to business. He had come, he said, to act in concert with the other "numerous armies and fleets which already display in every quarter of America the power, the justice, and, when properly sought, the mercy of the King." This was an interesting statement because it showed that the general was living in cloud cuckooland—he was under the firm impression that Howe was going to march *up* the Hudson to join him, and not go off in the *opposite* direction, to Philadelphia. Acting "in concert," of course, means acting *together*.

Burgoyne then went on to state the war aims for which British arms had been called into operation: to

John Burgoyne, from an engraving by A. H. Ritchie.

restore constitutional rule to a country from which it had been snatched by lawless rebellion. Sternly, he accused the rebels of practicing

arbitrary imprisonment, confiscation of property, persecution and torture, unprecedented in the inquisitions of the Romish Church. . . . These are inflicted by assemblies and committees, who dare to profess themselves friends to liberty, upon the most quiet subjects, without distinction of age or sex, for the sole crime . . . of having adhered in principle to the government under which they were born.

The British forces, he continued, had come to the colonies to provide security for life and property, not to plunder the innocent. "The domestic, the industrious, the infirm," wrote the general,

and even the timid inhabitants, I am desirous to protect, provided they remain quietly at their houses; that they do not suffer their cattle to be removed, nor their corn or forage to be secreted or destroyed; that they do not break up their bridges or roads; nor by any other act, directly or indirectly, endeavor to obstruct the operations of the King's troops, or supply or assist those of the enemy. Every species of provision brought to my camp, will be paid for at an equitable rate, in solid coin.

Ah, but if you distrusted these fine promises, and wanted no more of British rule? Let not such people, Burgoyne warned, think that distance would protect them. "I have but to give stretch to the Indian forces under my command, and they amount to thousands, to overtake the hardened enemies of Great Britain and

America. . . . The messengers of justice and of wrath await them in the field."

Thus wrote the general from Crown Point on June 30. He was promptly answered by Francis Hopkinson, a member of the Continental Congress in Philadelphia who ranks with Tom Paine as a master of revolutionary propaganda and satire.

What words [wrote Hopkinson] can express the pleni-tude of our horror, when the Colonel of the Queen's reg-iment of light dragoons advanced toward Ticonderoga? The mountains shook before thee, and the trees of the forest bowed their lofty heads; the vast lakes of the north were chilled at thy presence, and the mighty cataracts stopped their tremendous career, and were suspended in awe at thy approach. Judge then, oh ineffable Governor of Fort William in North Britain, what must have been the terror, dismay, and despair that overspread this paltry continent of America, and us its wretched inhabitants. Dark and dreary, indeed, was the prospect before us, till, like the sun in the horizons, your most gracious, sublime, and irresistible proclamation opened the doors of mercy, and snatched us, as it were, from the jaws of annihilation.

Hopkinson ridiculed Burgoyne's assertion that he had come to restore the constitution and the rule of law:

Is it for this, oh sublime lieutenant-general, that you have given yourself the trouble to cross the wide Atlantic, and with incredible fatigue traverse uncultivated wilds? And we ungratefully refuse the proferred blessings? To restore the rights of the constitution you have called together an amiable host of savages, and turned them loose to scalp

our women and children, and lay our country waste—
this they have performed with their usual skill and clem-
ency, and we yet remain insensible of the benefit, and
unthankful for so much goodness!

Who, asked Hopkinson in mock terror, could fail to
be convinced in an argument backed so persuasively by
the scalping knife and the bayonet? Withhold the messengers of wrath, he pleaded; do not give stretch to the
Indian restorers of constitutional rights. "We are *domestic*, we are *industrious*," he said,

we are infirm and timid; we shall remain quietly at home,
and not remove our cattle, or corn, or forage, in hopes
that you will come at the head of troops in the full pow-
ers of health, discipline, and valor, and take charge of
them for yourselves. Behold our wives and daughters, our
flocks and herds, our goods and chattels. Are they not at
the mercy of our Lord the King, and of his lieutenant-
general, member of the House of Commons, and governor of Fort William in North Britain?

The Yankees laughed long and loud at these irreverent
thrusts; but it soon became clear that Burgoyne meant
business. On July 5, 1777, General Arthur St. Clair, who
commanded at Ticonderoga, decided that he could not
defend the fort, and that to save his ragged, half-starved
garrison of 2,000 men he must withdraw at once. General
Simon Fraser, commanding the British Advance Corps,
followed in hot pursuit of the rebels, who fled in a
southeasterly direction down the road to Hubbardton.
The loss of Ticonderoga shocked Congress, and sent a
shiver of apprehension through the country. Only a

small band of Continentals and a handful of militia under the command of General Philip Schuyler stood between Burgoyne and Albany.

On July 8 Burgoyne began to concentrate his forces at Skenesborough, at the head of Lake Champlain, in preparation for his triumphal march south. At this very time, on the evening of July 10, a tiny band of American guerrillas carried out a daring raid across the waters of Narragansett Bay. Rhode Island militiamen, swooping down silently in the dead of night, captured Richard Prescott, the commander of the British occupation forces at Newport. They were seeking a fair exchange for General Charles Lee, who had been captured the previous December by the British in a New Jersey tavern.

The organizer of this coup was William Barton, a young colonel of militia from the town of Warren, Rhode Island, who was stationed at the Tiveston Heights emplacement overlooking Howland's Ferry. Some of the essential information that Barton needed came from a British deserter: British forces on Rhode Island, as everywhere else, were plagued by numerous desertions, and escape, in this case, was particularly easy. Men were always escaping from the post at Commonsense Point, on the northernmost tip of Rhode Island, from which the militia ferried them to the mainland. Lieutenant Frederick Mackenzie wrote somewhat plaintively, "As the rebels have small parties on the Neck [Commonsense Point] almost every night, and our deserters go immediately to the farthest point, it is very difficult to prevent them getting off."

From one of these deserters—probably a soldier of the

43rd Regiment who deserted on July 2—Barton received information that enabled him to make a plan to capture Prescott. The general, it seems, was in the habit of riding out every night to Mr. Overing's house four and a half miles north of Newport: there he relaxed after a busy day, and in the morning returned, refreshed, to town. He was, one might say, a commuter general. The Overing house was only three-quarters of a mile from the island's western shore.

Colonel Barton selected forty men and, in the words of the *Pennsylvania Evening Post,* "told them his design, acknowledged that it was hazardous, and probably could not be executed without the loss of life to some of those engaged in it; that he, for his part, was determined to risk his." All the militiamen elected to go with the colonel. Embarking in five open boats, they "set off with muffled oars, crossed the [Mount Hope] bay, passed Bristol Ferry, where the British have a fort, undiscovered," then rowed westward to Warwick Point and southward down Narragansett Bay. Coming out into the open waters west of Conanicut Point, they slipped between the men o' war anchored along the Rhode Island shore and landed about half a mile north of Weaver's Cove.

It was about eleven o'clock in the evening as Colonel Barton led the way inland, with two black soldiers right behind him. What happened is described in the report of the *Pennsylvania Evening Post:*

A single sentinel saw and hailed the colonel; he answered by exclaiming against and inquiring for rebel prisoners,

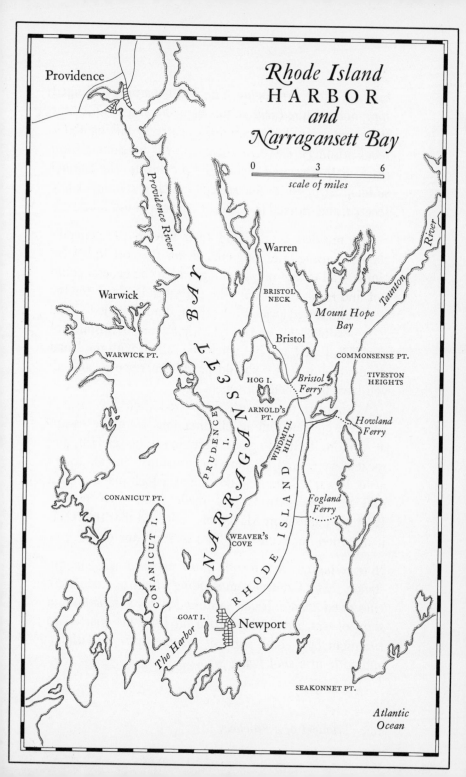

Providence

Rhode Island
HARBOR
and
Narragansett Bay

0   3   6
scale of miles

Providence River

Warren

BRISTOL
NECK

*Mount Hope
Bay*

Warwick

Taunton River

WARWICK PT.

Bristol

COMMONSENSE PT.

HOG I.

*Bristol
Ferry*

TIVESTON
HEIGHTS

ARNOLD'S
PT.

*Howland
Ferry*

WINDMILL HILL

CONANICUT PT.

*Fogland
Ferry*

WEAVER'S
COVE

RHODE ISLAND

GOAT I.

Newport

SEAKONNET PT.

The Harbor

*Atlantic
Ocean*

but kept slowly advancing. The sentinel again challenged him, and required the countersign; he said he had not the countersign, but amused the sentry by talking about rebel prisoners, and still advancing till he came within reach of the bayonet, which, he presenting, the colonel suddenly struck aside and seized him. He was immediately secured, and ordered to be silent, on pain of instant death.

The invaders soon found their way to the general's room. Waiting only long enough for Prescott to get his clothes—all except one stocking, which the general could not find in his confusion—the party headed back for the beach and rowed away. Prescott sat, dumbfounded. "And is it possible," he exclaimed, "that I am a prisoner of war! Yes, I see I am; but when you set out with me I had no doubt but that I should have been rescued, and all you have been made prisoners."

As soon as the British discovered their loss, search parties were sent out in all directions from the camps at Windmill Hill, Fogland Ferry, and Quaker Hill, and rockets were fired to alert the warships; but all to no avail. It was a dark, moonless night, which made pursuit difficult. The patriots had made good their escape. Ruefully Lieutenant Mackenzie conceded that the rebels had carried out their raid "in a masterly manner."

It is certainly [he wrote] a most extraordinary circumstance, that a General commanding a body of 4,000 men, encamped on an Island surrounded by a squadron of ships of war, should be carried off from his quarters in the night by a small party of the enemy from without, and without a shot being fired.

Clearly the Americans possessed far more information than they could have obtained from deserters alone. The incident, Mackenzie thought,

> is a convincing proof that the enemy receive from some of the inhabitants of this Island, the most perfect intelligence of every circumstance of which they wish to be informed. Some of those concerned in the execution of it, knew the ground perfectly well . . . and they must have been thoroughly well informed of the positions of the guards and sentries, as they could not possibly have come a nearer, or a better way to the house.

While this was going on, General Burgoyne was at Skenesborough, poised with an army 10,000 strong for his triumphal march to the Hudson. Gentleman Johnny had a low opinion of his enemy, and as yet no doubt had entered his mind that he would soon be a victorious hero; but the farther south he went, the tougher the going became. After the first shock of Ticonderoga, the American soldiers exchanged their guns for axes and went to work with a will, felling the tall pines across the forest road down which Burgoyne must advance to Fort Edward, breaking the bridges, flooding the path, and scorching the earth. Slowly Burgoyne's engineers cleared away the roadblocks, and the long column of blue- and red-clad soldiers shuffled on toward the Hudson. Burgoyne reached the river at Fort Edward on July 29 and set up his headquarters there.

As the British inched forward, the armies coming up against them were swelling. Matters were helped on by Burgoyne's Indian allies, to whom he had "given stretch" with instructions to loot and murder rebels but to spare women, children, and the aged. In the village of Argyle, north of Fort Edward, the inhabitants were fleeing before Burgoyne's Indian scouts. What happened there on July 26 to Janie McCrea, as she waited for her lover David, a loyalist lieutenant, was reported in a dispatch to the *Pennsylvania Evening Post* on July 27 and published on August 12:

General Burgoyne is at Fort Edward. Frequent injuries and horrible actions committed by his scouting parties of Indians on single unarmed men and defenseless women, are sufficient to give every man a thorough detestation of their whole conduct. . . . One instance, which happened yesterday, during a skirmish, may serve for the whole. A young lady, by the name of Miss Jenny M'Crea, of a good family, and some share of beauty, was, by some accident, at Ford Edward when the enemy attacked the picket guard. She and an old woman were taken by the savages, who generally serve as an advance guard or flanking parties to the Regulars . . . and then, with a barbarity unheard of before, they butchered the poor innocent girl, and scalped her. . . . What renders this affair more remarkable is, that Miss M'Crea has a brother an officer in the British service, now at New York, and she herself leaned to that side of the question; but thus they treat their friends as well as their enemies.

The militia of the surrounding region had begun to embody when news came of Burgoyne's invasion. Janie McCrea's murder added zest and speed to the process. When John Stark, veteran of the New Jersey campaign,

Needlepoint, Newburyport, Massachusetts, 1767.

received a commission in July from New Hampshire to organize a militia brigade, men flocked to his standard. With Seth Warner's Vermont militia, Stark by mid-August commanded nearly 2,000 New England volunteers.

At Bennington, Vermont, on August 16 Stark ran smack into a foraging party of German regulars under Colonels Baum and Breymann, and totally defeated them in two encounters on that day. Bennington was a patriot supply center, and there were many horses there. Burgoyne desperately needed horses to bring his supplies up from Fort George: he instructed Baum "to bring in one thousand three hundred horses at least, with all the saddles and bridles that can be found, together with all the wagons, carriages, draft oxen, and cattle fit for slaughter." We note—in the light of Burgoyne's previous promises—that Baum received no instructions to pay for what he took. The defeat of the German looting expedition, therefore, was a twofold blow: it denied Burgoyne the supplies he needed, and reduced his army by a thousand men wounded, captured, or dead. An American correspondent writing of the engagement in the *Pennsylvania Evening Post* on September 4 came to the conclusion that "if a large body of militia was now called to act in conjunction with the northern army, the enemy might be entirely overthrown." Here he stated a lesson central for the proper conduct of people's wars: victory depends upon the correct, coordinated use of regular troops and irregular (militia) forces.

One of the top commanders of the German troops with Burgoyne was General Friedrich Riedesel. For him

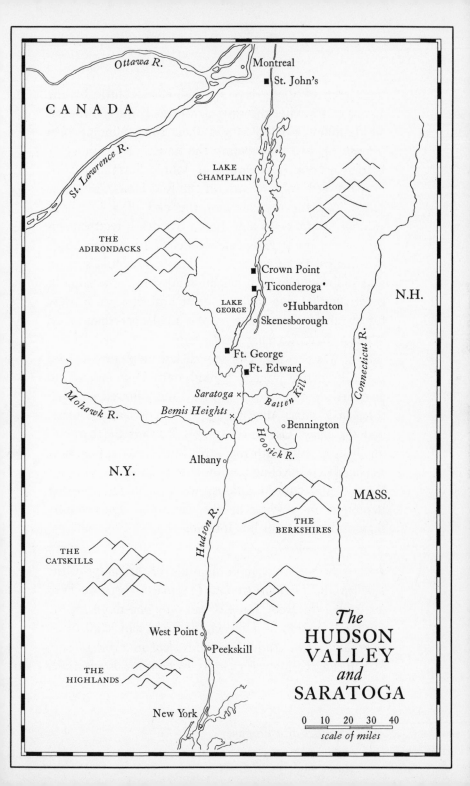

Ottawa R.

Montreal
St. John's

CANADA

St. Lawrence R.

LAKE
CHAMPLAIN

THE
ADIRONDACKS

N.H.

Crown Point
Ticonderoga
LAKE
GEORGE
Hubbardton
Skenesborough

Ft. George
Ft. Edward

Mohawk R.

Saratoga ×
Bemis Heights ×

Batten Kill

Bennington

Hoosick R.

Albany

N.Y.

Connecticut R.

MASS.

THE
BERKSHIRES

THE
CATSKILLS

Hudson R.

West Point
Peekskill

THE
HIGHLANDS

New York

The
HUDSON
VALLEY
and
SARATOGA

0 10 20 30 40
scale of miles

the gloom of these days was lightened a little by the arrival of his wife, the tiny, dark-haired, thirty-one-year-old Baroness Frederika, and their three children. On August 14, two days before the battle of Bennington, Frederika took up quarters at John's Farm, north of Fort Edward. John's Farm, or the Red House, as it was called, was for the baroness the end of a long and arduous journey. When Baron Riedesel received his commission in 1776 as commander of Brunswick forces in America, there was no question in Frederika's mind that she would go with her husband; for, as she said, "it is certain that one suffers a great deal more in anxiety for an absent loved one who is in danger than when one can share the danger with him."

So it was decided. The general left Germany in April 1776; Frederika waited behind only long enough to give birth to a daughter, and then she followed with her three little girls: Augusta, age six; Frederika, age three; and the baby, Caroline. At Fort Edward the baroness finally caught up with the army. Since leaving Germany she had been traveling four months in difficult and sometimes dangerous conditions; we can understand her happiness in arriving at the Hudson. "The country there," she wrote in her *Journal*,

was lovely, and we were in the midst of the camps of the English and German troops. The place where we lived was called the Red House. I had only one room for my husband, myself, and my children, in which all of us slept, and a tiny study. My maids slept in a sort of hall. When the weather was good we had our meals out under *the trees, otherwise we had them in a barn, laying boards across barrels for tables. It was here I ate bear meat for the first time, and it tasted very good to me. Sometimes we had nothing at all, but in spite of everything I was happy and satisfied, for I was with my children and beloved by all about me.*

Thus the hot August days passed as Burgoyne waited for his supplies to build up. Early in September he decided to move on; he put his army across the Hudson at Batten Kill and moved south down the river road toward Saratoga. His forces had shrunk to not much more than 6,000 men. As for the American forces, they were growing all the time. A New Englander, Horatio Gates, had now been placed in charge of them. Gates had at his disposal a hard core of Continental troops, perhaps 3,000, and nearly three times that number of militia, who continued to pour in from Connecticut, Massachusetts, New Hampshire, New York, and Vermont.

Baroness Frederika also took to the road, in the coach with her children and maids. Burgoyne was reluctant to give the authorization: he knew by now that he was in deep trouble, with no hope of assistance from Howe, his Indian allies gone, and the enemy in front of him and at his rear. But Frederika insisted. Many women followed their men to war—there were hundreds of them with the British troops—so why not she? "We had," she recalled, "high hopes of victory . . . and when we crossed the Hudson and General Burgoyne said Britons never retreat, we were all in high spirits."

To halt Burgoyne's advance, Gates followed the guidance of his Polish adviser, the wise Kosciusko. He entrenched his forces on Bemis Heights, a thickly wooded plateau that dominated the narrow road between the hills and the river. Here was joined, on September 19, the first battle of Bemis Heights, otherwise known as the battle of Freeman's Farm. General Riedesel, commanding the British left, advanced down the river road; some way behind him rode the baroness and her children in the coach. "I followed the army right in the midst of the soldiers, who sang and were jolly, burning with the desire for victory," the baroness wrote. "We passed through endless woods, and the country was magnificent, but completely deserted." The inhabitants, of course, had fled, and the men had joined the militia. "This was a great disadvantage to us, because every inhabitant is a born soldier and a good marksman; in addition, the thought of fighting for their country and for freedom made them braver than ever."

Burgoyne's men attacked Gates's entrenchments bravely, but gained in the end nothing but hundreds wounded, captured, or dead. The British withdrew and dug in, hoping that help would come from Sir Henry Clinton in New York. A vain hope! Clinton did, it is true, create a diversion on October 5 by storming and taking Forts Clinton and Montgomery on the Hudson River opposite Peekskill; but he came no farther. And, in the meantime, Burgoyne's position grew worse with every passing hour. John Stark and the New Hampshire militia sat astride the British communications line between Fort George and Fort Edward, and forces from Massachusetts were moving in from the west to cross the Hudson and bar the British retreat north of Saratoga.

Riedesel and other officers urged Burgoyne to go back to Ticonderoga while yet he might, and winter there; but Gentleman Johnny insisted on making one last stab at the enemy. Thus was fought, on October 7, the senseless and wasteful second battle of Bemis Heights. On that day Baroness Frederika had planned a dinner party for her husband and his colleagues, Generals Simon Fraser, William Phillips, and John Burgoyne himself. In midafternoon, when the table was already set, Frederika received a rude surprise. Simon Fraser was carried in gravely wounded. Mounted on his great gray charger, he had been in the thick of the battle, gallantly stemming an American attack on the British center, when one of Morgan's riflemen picked him off.

"The table," said the baroness, "which had already been set for dinner, was removed, and a bed for the general put in its place. I sat in a corner of the room, shivering and trembling. The noise of the firing grew constantly louder. The thought that perhaps my husband would also be brought home wounded was terrifying and worried me incessantly." Amid his agony Fraser kept moaning "Oh, fatal ambition! Poor General Burgoyne! Poor Mrs. Fraser." By now Frederika was almost hysterical with grief and fright, and soon the whole house was filled with wounded and dying men. But the return of her husband calmed her. Later she put the children to bed, and passed a sleepless night, "constantly afraid that my children might wake up and cry, thus disturbing the poor dying man, who kept apologizing for causing me so much trouble."

Baroness Frederika von Riedesel.

Early in the morning of October 8 the end came. Burgoyne, who now knew only too well that he was beaten and must retreat, waited long enough to bury his friend. Sergeant Roger Lamb described the scene:

About sunset the corpse was carried up the hill. The procession was in view of both armies. As it passed by, Generals Burgoyne, Phillips, and Riedesel, with most of the officers of the army, joined the procession. The troops who fought immediately under General Fraser . . . urged by a natural wish to pay the last honors to him in the eyes of the whole army, marched after the body in solemn procession to the grave.

As the cannon thundered and the balls whistled over the heads of the mourners, chaplain Edward Brudenel read the service for the dead.

Then it began to rain in a steady downpour. The sodden army turned in its tracks and plodded back along the road by which it had come. But Burgoyne had waited too long before making his decision: by October 13 he was surrounded on all sides and exposed to the merciless bombardment of Gates's cannon; provisions were almost gone. There was nothing to do but negotiate surrender.

While the talks went on, the soldiers of the two armies began to fraternize with one another and exchange greetings across the Hudson River. What happened then is described by Roger Lamb:

A soldier in the 9th regiment, named Maguire, came down to the river with a number of his companions, who engaged in conversation with a party of Americans on the opposite shore. . . . Maguire suddenly darted like light-

ning from his companions, and resolutely plunged into the stream. At the very same moment, one of the American soldiers, seized with a similar impulse, dashed into the water from the opposite shore. The wondering soldiers on both sides beheld them eagerly swim toward the middle of the river, where they met. They hung on each other's necks, and wept: and the loud cries of "my brother, my dear brother!" which accompanied the transaction, soon cleared up the mystery to the astonished spectators.

On October 17 the British laid down their arms at Saratoga and marched to the American camp, into the presence of their enemies. Three years later the Marquis de Chastellux, a French general, visited this spot. "I confess," said he,

> that when I was conducted to the spot where the British laid down their arms . . . I shared the triumph of the Americans, and at the same time admired their nobility and magnanimity; for the soldiers and officers beheld their presumptuous and sanguinary enemies pass, without offering the smallest insult, without suffering an insulting smile or gesture to escape them. This majestic silence offered a striking refutation of the vain declamations of the English general.

Then Baroness Frederika drove into the American camp with her children. "I was comforted," she said, "to note that nobody glanced at us insultingly, that they all bowed to me, and some of them even looked with pity to see a woman with small children there." General Schuyler, whose mansion at Schuylerville Burgoyne had burned to the ground during the retreat a few days earlier, invited the lady to his tent. "A very handsome man," she wrote, "came towards me, lifted the children out of the calash, and kissed them, and then, with tears in his eyes, helped me out." Then they all went to supper. "He treated me," wrote Frederika, "to delicious smoked tongue, beefsteaks, potatoes, and good bread and butter. No dinner had ever tasted better to me. I was content. I saw that all about me were likewise, and, most important of all, my husband was out of danger."

As soon as he could, amid the press of business, Horatio Gates sat down to write to his wife and son.

The voice of fame ere this reaches you will tell how greatly fortunate we have been in this department. Burgoyne and his whole army have laid down their arms and surrendered themselves to me and my Yankees. . . . Tell my dear Bob not to be too elated at this great good fortune of his father. He and I have seen days adverse, as well as prosperous. Let us through life endeavor to bear both with an equal mind.

From October 17 until the end of the month Lieutenant Frederick Mackenzie, on Rhode Island, was very busy with preparations to repulse a rumored invasion by 10,000 New England militia. He did not learn about Burgoyne's surrender until October 31, when the excitement had subsided and he found time to read the American newspapers that had just been brought in. The bumpkins who had arrested General Prescott in the very bosom of the British forces had now whisked away, not one man, but an entire army.

Lieutenant Frederick Mackenzie was speechless.

General Burgoyne's Surrender

When‿ Jack, the King's com‿man‿der‿ bold, Was
go - ing to‿ his‿ du - ty, Through‿
all the crowd he smiled‿ and‿ bow'd To
ev' - ry bloom - ing beau - ty. The
cit - y rung with feats he'd done In
Por - tu - gal and Flan - ders, And‿
all the town thought he'd‿ be‿ crown'd The
first of Al - ex - an - ders.

To Hampton Court he first repairs,
  To kiss great George's hand, sirs,
Then to harangue on state affairs,
  Before he left the land, sirs.
The Lower House sat mute as mouse
  To hear his grand oration;
And all the peers with loudest cheers
  Proclaimed him to the nation.

Then off he went to Canada,
  Next to Ticonderoga,
And quitting those, away he goes,
  Straightway to Saratoga.
With great parade his march he made,
  To gain his wished-for station,
When far and wide his minions hied,
  To spread his "Proclamation."

To such as stayed he offers made,
  Of "pardon on submission;
But savage bands should waste the lands
  Of all in opposition."
But ah, the cruel fate of war!
  This boasted son of Britain,
When mounting his triumphal car,
  With sudden fear was smitten.

The sons of freedom gathered round,
  His hostile bands confounded,
And when they'd fain have turn'd their backs,
  They found themselves surrounded!
In vain they fought, in vain they fled,
  Their chief, humane and tender,
To save the rest, soon thought it best
  His forces to surrender.

THE COLD GROUND
Valley Forge, 1777–1778

May we still be found,
Content with our hard fate, my boys,
On the cold, cold ground.

"How Stands the Glass Around?"

At the very time, June 30, 1777, that Burgoyne appeared at Crown Point and penned his pompous declaration, General Sir William Howe was withdrawing his troops from New Jersey and ferrying them over from Amboy to Staten Island. To Washington, whose headquarters were then at Morristown, New Jersey, the movement that Billy Howe had in mind was as obvious as it was inevitable. "I had no doubt in my own mind," wrote George Washington, "but that General Howe would push up the [Hudson] river, to cooperate with General Burgoyne." Washington saw himself faced with the unenviable task of moving his tatterdemalion army up to the highlands between New York City and Albany to block the British advance.

But what Washington expected never happened. On

July 24 the American commander-in-chief learned, to his stupefaction, that the British army and the British navy, with all the King's horses as well as his men, had put out to sea and gone off no one knew where!

As a matter of fact, Billy Howe had begun to embark his troops on the transports at the beginning of July; but the armada did not weigh anchor and sail from Sandy Hook until July 23. It was a magnificent and awe-inspiring scene, 260 tall ships moving in silence amid a cloud of billowing white canvas. Four days later the fleet was sighted off the capes of Delaware Bay; it became clear that Philadelphia was Howe's objective.

Reluctantly, because he feared that the whole thing was a trick, Washington moved his army southward; he reached Philadelphia on July 31. There he met a young Frenchman who had just arrived in town, burning with enthusiasm to serve the revolutionary cause. This youth, whose name was Marie-Jean-Paul, had charmed Congress into commissioning him as a major-general. He would later serve throughout the Pennsylvania campaign and pass the winter with the troops at Valley Forge. Washington, who had no children of his own, conceived an instant affection for the young man and came to think of him as his own son. Marie-Jean-Paul was wealthy in his own right, and possessed a French title of nobility—the Marquis de Lafayette. When, in 1776, news of the Revolution had reached him in France, he bought and equipped a ship, and sailed off to America in defiance of the order of his king, Louis XVI. Lafayette left behind a wife and two small children, to whom he wrote, "From love of me become a good American. The

The Marquis de Lafayette,
by Charles Wilson Peale (1741-1847).

welfare of America is closely bound up with the welfare of mankind."

Late in August, while Washington and Lafayette were examining Philadelphia's defenses and preparing for the struggle that loomed ahead, Billy Howe began to land his men on the west bank of the Elk River, which flows into Chesapeake Bay on the northeastern side. The British troops had been at sea for five weeks amid sickness, stifling heat, boredom and inactivity—some of them, indeed, had been sweating on the transports for nearly two months. As for the poor horses, dozens had died and been thrown overboard.

General Sir William Howe, like his colleague Burgoyne, began his campaign with a proclamation "given under my hand at head-quarters of the Army, the 27th day of August, 1777." Howe assured "peaceable inhabitants" and "well-disposed subjects" that

he hath issued the strictest Orders to his Troops for the preservation of Regularity and Good Discipline, and has signified that the most exemplary Punishment shall be inflicted upon Those who shall dare to plunder the Property, or molest the Persons of any of his Majesty's well-disposed subjects.

Howe had good reason to worry about the behavior of his troops. News of Hessian and British ravages in New Jersey had spread far and wide, contributing to the speed and bitterness with which people in that state had turned to resistance. During the retreat from New

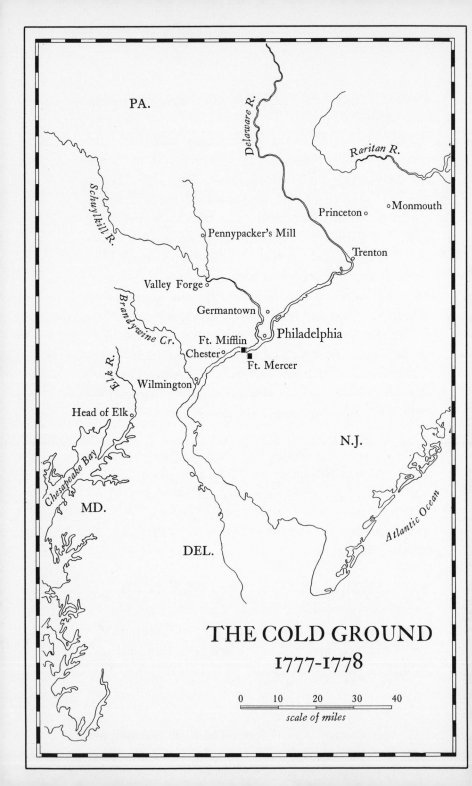

PA.

Delaware R.

Raritan R.

Schuylkill R.

Princeton ○　　○ Monmouth

○ Pennypacker's Mill

Trenton

Valley Forge ○

Brandywine Cr.

Germantown ○

Ft. Mifflin
Chester ○ □
Ft. Mercer

Philadelphia

Elk R.

Wilmington ○

Head of Elk ○

N.J.

Chesapeake Bay

MD.

DEL.

Atlantic Ocean

THE COLD GROUND
1777-1778

0　　10　　20　　30　　40

scale of miles

Jersey in June, a young English captain, John Andre, had noted regretfully in his *Journal* that "the spirit of depredation was but too prevalent on these marches . . . We scarcely met a man at home excepting the old and infirm." And, on the very day that the British landed on the Elk, Ambrose Serle, one of Howe's own staff officers, wrote bitterly that "the Hessians are more infamous and cruel than any. It is a misfortune we ever had such a dirty, cowardly set of contemptible miscreants."

John Andre, the captain who recorded with care the movement of the British army on its way to Philadelphia, was a young man about twenty-six years old who possessed, like Lafayette, brilliant talent and extraordinary personal charm. He spoke French, German, and Italian as well as his native English; he was a musician and writer. But Andre's only ambition was to be a soldier, and he had joined the British army in 1771. When he landed on the banks of the Elk River, he was aide-de-camp to the British general, Charles Grey.

In spite of Howe's promises, the troops began to plunder as soon as they landed. "There was a good deal of plunder committed by the troops, notwithstanding the strictest prohibitions," Captain Andre wrote in his *Journal* on August 26. "No method was fixed yet for supplying the troops with fresh provisions in a regular manner. The soldiers slaughtered a good deal of cattle clandestinely." In any event, Howe's promise of immunity was directed only at the "peaceable and well-disposed." As the inhabitants fled before him, he sent

Major John Andre,
from an engraving by W. G. Jackman.

out foraging parties to drive in their cattle and seize the supplies he needed. Some soldiers, it is true, were flogged and a few hanged when they plundered not for the army's benefit but for their own private purposes. Howe felt that the army alone, not the individual soldiers, should be the recipient of stolen American goods.

As Howe's forces marched overland toward Philadelphia, Washington brought his troops down to Brandywine Creek, southwest of the city, to block the British advance. There, on September 11, he fought a defensive action, then fell back. Two weeks later a British contingent under the Earl of Cornwallis occupied Philadelphia and placed Forts Mifflin and Mercer, commanding the Delaware River approach, under blockade. A British officer wrote on September 26:

This morning the British and Hessian grenadiers under the command of Lord Cornwallis, preceded by six medium twelve pounders and four royal howitzers, marched in a kind of procession (with bands of music playing before them), and took possession of the city of Philadelphia. . . . This city is large, the streets spacious and regularly laid out, at right angles, and parallel to each other, which together with the houses being built of good colored bricks, gives it a very neat appearance in general. Its situation, however, so closely pent up as it is between two fresh-water rivers [the Delaware and the Schuylkill] makes it unhealthy. The usual number of inhabitants are estimated at 33,000, one-third of which are said to have evacuated the city on various accounts.

The city submitted to British occupation without disorder. "The fine appearance of the soldiery," wrote the loyalist *Rivington's Gazette*, "the strictness of their discipline, the politeness of the officers, and the orderly behavior of the whole body, immediately dispelled every apprehension of the inhabitants." But almost at once, on September 28, the cannon began to thunder at the American camp twenty miles away at Pennypacker's Mill when news arrived that Burgoyne had been thrown back at the first battle of Bemis Heights. "Deserters," wrote John Andre on September 30, "related that on the 28th Major Washington fired a *feu de joie* [victory salute] and administered rum to his army, on account of a victory gained over General Burgoyne."

On October 4 Washington delivered a surprise attack upon the main British forces that were encamped outside Philadelphia, in the village of Germantown. He was thrown back with heavy losses, but the attack gave spirit to his weary, hungry, rain-sodden troops. Then on October 18 the American cannon thundered again, and the sound was heard in Philadelphia, and the British troops did not have to ask, why the cannon thundered: "This," Andre wrote, "was a *feu de joie* on account of the taking of General Burgoyne and the Northern Army."

Early in December, Washington withdrew his ragged troops into winter quarters at Valley Forge, on the wooded slopes of the Schuylkill eighteen miles from Philadelphia. There the patriots would keep watch on Howe through the long winter months. They would freeze and starve amid the silence and the snow; many would die. As new graves appeared in the frozen earth, the soldiers would sing a British song telling of the desolation of a soldier's life.

How Stands the Glass Around?

Voice

(Guitar Instrumental)

How stands the glass around? For shame, ye take no care, my boys. How stands the glass a - round? Let mirth and wine a -

Why, soldiers, why,
Should we be melancholy, boys?
Why, soldiers, why,
Whose business 'tis to die!
What sighing, fie!
Drown fear, drink on, be jolly, boys,
'Tis he, you or I!
Cold, hot, wet or dry,
We're always bound to follow, boys,
And scorn to fly!

'Tis but in vain—
I mean not to upbraid ye, boys—
'Tis but in vain
For soldiers to complain.
Should next campaign
Send us to Him who made us, boys,
We're free from pain!
But if we remain,
A bottle and kind landlady
Cure all again.

The sufferings and life of the common soldier at this time come to us from the pen of one of them, Joseph Martin, a New Englander who was seventeen years old when he came to Valley Forge as a private in the 8th Connecticut Regiment. After the battle of Germantown, Martin's regiment saw action in the defense of Fort Mifflin, on Port Island in the Delaware. "Here," Martin recalled, "I endured hardships sufficient to kill a dozen horses . . . without provisions, without clothing, not a scrap of either shoes or stockings to my feet or legs, and in this condition to endure a siege in such a place as that was appalling in the highest degree."

The British onslaught on the fort reached its climax

on November 15 with a bombardment from the men o' war *Vigilant, Somerset, Isis, Roebuck,* and *Pearl,* stationed opposite the fort in the Delaware River. "Nearly every gun in the fort," wrote Martin,

was silenced by midday. Our men were cut up like cornstalks . . . As soon as it was dark we began to make preparations for evacuating the fort, and endeavoring to escape to the Jersey shore. When the firing had in some measure subsided and I could look about me, I found the fort exhibited a picture of desolation. The whole area was as completely ploughed as a field, the buildings of every kind hanging in broken fragments, and the guns all dismounted; and how many of the garrison sent to the world of spirits, I knew not. If ever destruction was complete, it was here. The surviving part of the garrison were now drawn off, and such of the stores as could conveniently be taken away were carried to the Jersey shore.

The 8th Connecticut marched off in the damp November weather to rejoin the main army, sleeping uncovered in the pelting rain, wolfing their meat raw when they were too tired or too wet to build fires. "The leaves and the ground," said Martin of one bivouac, "were as wet as water could make them. It was then foggy, and the water dropping from the trees like a shower. We endeavored to get fire by flashing powder on the leaves, but this and every other expedient that we could employ failing, we were forced by our old master, necessity, to lay down and sleep if we could, with three other of our constant companions, fatigue, hunger, and cold."

Martin and his companions had survived one of the

most heroic but little-known struggles of the entire war. Joining the grand army in time for Thanksgiving, the men dined off rice and toasted their country with a spoonful of vinegar apiece. Soon they trudged off to winter quarters. "We arrived at the Valley Forge in the evening," Martin wrote. "It was dark; there was no water to be found and I was weary and came to my tent without finding any. Fatigue and thirst, joined with hunger, almost made me desperate." Not only were the men hungry and thirsty but, almost literally, naked.

The greatest part were not only shirtless and barefoot, but destitute of all other clothing, especially blankets. I procured a small piece of cowhide and made myself a pair of moccasins, which kept my feet (while they lasted) from the frozen ground, although, as I well remember, the hard edges so galled my ankles, while on the march, that it was with much difficulty and pain that I could wear them afterwards; but the only alternative I had was to endure this inconvenience or go barefoot, as hundreds of my companions had to, till they might be tracked by their blood upon the rough, frozen ground.

Hunger, nakedness, and cold were only the beginning for Washington's soldiers. "We had hard duty to perform," said Martin, "and little or no strength to perform it with." The first of such duties when arriving at winter quarters was to erect huts. The ground was marked out by the quartermaster, then the soldiers must go and cut timber from the forest, using whatever tools they might beg, borrow, or steal. The timber being cut and notched, the huts were laid out, about twelve by fifteen feet, and the whole was roofed with shingles tied with straw onto a supporting frame of poles. A stone chimney, built into the middle of one side and sealed with clay or mud, completed the shelter. For floor and bed the men had native Pennsylvania dirt. For bedding, straw or sometimes a thin blanket.

The Pennsylvania countryside was rich in farms and crops, but the roads were few and bad; if Washington's troops were to eat, they would have to procure supplies even as the British had procured them, by scouring the countryside, driving in the cattle and sheep, and hauling flour with their own wagons. Private Martin was employed in this business of foraging from the time of his arrival at Valley Forge until the following April, and this gave him some relief from the cold monotony of camp life. The mission, he stated bluntly, was "nothing more or less than to procure provisions from the inhabitants for the men in the army and forage for the poor perishing cattle belonging to it, at the point of the bayonet."

But use of the bayonet evidently was not necessary. From what Martin says, the people offered little resistance to the foraging. "I do not remember that during the time I was employed in this business . . . ever to have met with the least resistance from the inhabitants, take what we would from their barns, mills, corncribs, or stalls." This, it seems, was true, with one exception: the people objected to the removal of their horses.

When we came to their stables, then look out for the women. Take what horse you would, it was one or the other's "pony" and they had no other to ride to church. And when we had got possession of a horse we were sure to have half a dozen or more women pressing upon us, until by some means or other, if possible, they would slip the bridle from the horse's head, and then we might catch him again if we could. They would take no more notice of a charged bayonet than a blind horse would of a cocked pistol. It would answer no purpose to threaten to kill them with the bayonet or musket; they knew as well as we did that we would not put our threats into execution; and when they had thus liberated a horse (which happened but seldom) they would laugh at us and ask why we did not do as we threatened, kill them, and then they would generally ask us into their houses and treat us with as much kindness as though nothing had happened.

Thus we see that life at Valley Forge was not a bad one for those who went frequently on foraging expeditions. Private Martin's *Narrative* tells eloquently of the intolerable sufferings undergone through six years of war, but he complains little of the winter of 1777–1778. "We fared much better than I had ever done in the army before," he wrote,

or ever did afterwards. We had very good provisions all winter and generally enough of them. Some of us were constantly in the country with the wagons; we went out by turns and had no one to control us . . . When we were in the country we were pretty sure to fare well, for the inhabitants were remarkably kind to us. We had no guards to keep, our only duty was to help load the wagons with hay, corn, meal, or whatever they were to take off, *and when they were thus loaded, to keep them company til they arrived at the commissary's.*

When not on such duties as building fortifications or huts, lumbering, guard, or foraging, the men were constantly engaged in "learning the Baron de Steuben's new Prussian exercise. It was a continual drill." Frederick von Steuben was a Prussian officer who arrived at Valley Forge in February 1778 and was at once given the assignment of drilling and disciplining the troops. He worked out a drill system and taught drillmasters; soon he had the whole army marching and practicing the manual of arms.

Tory wits in Philadelphia found the spectacle amusing. "Come Out Ye Continentalers," probably composed in 1778, mocked the efforts of Washington's drillmasters to make regular soldiers out of country bumpkins.

Come Out Ye Continentalers

Come out ye Continentalers,
We're going for to go,
To fight the redcoat enemy,
Who're plaguey cute, you know, my boys,
Who're plaguey cute, you know.

Fix bayonets! That's your sort, my boys,
Now quick time march! that's right!
Just so we'd poke the enemy
If they were but in sight, my boys,
If they were but in sight.

Halt! Shoulder whoop! Stop laughing, Nick!
By platoons wheel, right dress!
Hold up your muzzles on the left.
No talking—more or less—my boys,
No talking more or less.

Bill Sneezer keep your canteen down,
We're going for to travel.
"Captain, I wants to halt a bit,
My shoes are full of gravel, sir,
My shoes are full of gravel."

Ho! Strike up music! Forward march!
Come point your toes, Bob Rogers.
See, yonder come the redcoat men!
Let's fly upon them soldiers, boys,
Let's fly upon them soldiers.

Just before Steuben's arrival the Continental troops had had a little fun of their own. The captain under whom Joseph Martin served in the 8th Connecticut was David Bushnell, a Yankee inventor whose one-man submarine had caused a sensation when tested on the Hudson in 1776. While at Valley Forge the ingenious captain filled a number of kegs with gunpowder, set fuses to them, and sent them floating downriver in the hope that they would bump into the British men o' war anchored downstream. What happened on January 5 was gleefully related by a Philadelphia correspondent of the *New Jersey Gazette* on January 21: "Some time last week," he wrote,

two boys observed a keg of a singular construction, floating in the river opposite to the city; they got into a small boat, and attempting to take up the keg, it burst with a great explosion, and blew up the unfortunate boys. Yesterday, several kegs of a like construction made their appearance. An alarm was immediately spread through the city; various reports prevailed, filling the city and the royal troops with consternation. Some reported that the kegs were filled with armed rebels, who were to issue forth in the dead of night, as the Grecians did of old from their wooden horse at the siege of Troy, and take the city by surprise; asserting that they had seen the points of their bayonets through the bungholes of the kegs. Others said they were charged with the most inveterate combustibles, to be kindled by secret machinery, and setting the whole Delaware in flames, were to consume all the shipping in the harbor; whilst others asserted that they were constructed by . . . magic, would of themselves ascend the wharves in the night time, and roll all flaming through the streets of the city, destroying every thing in their way. The shipping in the harbor, and all the wharves in the city were fully manned, the battle began, and it was surprising to behold the incessant blaze that was kept up against the enemy, the kegs. Both officers and men exhibited the most unparalleled skill and bravery on the occasion; whilst the citizens stood gazing as solemn witnesses of their prowess. From the Roebuck and other ships of war, whole broadsides were poured into the Delaware. In short, not a wandering ship, stick, or drift log, but felt the vigor of the British arms.

The loyalist *Pennsylvania Ledger* pooh-poohed the whole affair. Conceding that some barrels "of odd appearance" had come floating down the Delaware, "a few guns," said the writer casually, "were, we believe, fired at them from some of the transports lying along the wharves. Other than this no notice was taken of them."

But the opportunity to deride the British was too good to miss. The "battle of the kegs," as it was ever after known, was immortalized by that same Francis Hopkinson whom we first met pouring ridicule on Burgoyne's proclamation. His ballad, "Battle of the Kegs," set all America laughing and even warmed the soldiers shivering around the campfires of Valley Forge.

Battle of the Kegs

TUNE: YANKEE DOODLE

Gal - lants at - tend, and hear a friend Trill forth har - mon - ious dit - ty: Strange things I'll tell, which late be - fell In Phil - a - del - phia ci - ty. 'Twas

ear - ly day, as po - ets say, Just when the sun was
ris - ing, A sol - dier stood on a
log of wood And saw a thing sur - pris - ing.

As in a maze, he stood to gaze,
    The truth can't be denied, sir,
He spy'd a score—of kegs, or more,
    Come floating down the tide, sir.
A sailor too, in jerkin blue,
    The strange appearance viewing,

First damn'd his eyes, in great surprise,
    Then said some mischief's brewing.

These kegs now hold the rebels bold,
    Pack'd up like pickled herring:
And they're come down t'attack the town,
    In this new way of ferrying.
The soldier flew, the sailor too,
    And, scar'd almost to death, sir,
Wore out their shoes, to spread the news,
    And ran till out of breath, sir.

Now up and down, throughout the town,
    Most frantic scenes were acted:
And some ran here, and some ran there
    Like men almost distracted.
Some fire cry'd, which some deny'd,
    But said the earth had quaked:
And girls and boys, with hideous noise,
    Ran through the town half naked.

Sir William he, snug as a flea,
    Lay all this time a-snoring,
Nor dreamt of harm, as he lay warm
    In bed with Mrs. L[orin]g.
Now in affright, he starts upright,
    Awak'd by such a clatter;
He rubs both eyes and boldly cries,
    "For God's sake, what's the matter?"

At his bedside, he then espy'd
    Sir Erskine at command, sir,
Upon one foot he had one boot,
    And t'other in his hand, sir.
"Arise! Arise!" Sir Erskine cries:
    "The rebels—more's the pity—
Without a boat, are all on float,
    And rang'd before the city.

"The motley crew, in vessels new,
    With Satan for their guide, sir,
Pack'd up in bags, or wooden kegs,
    Come driving down the tide, sir.
Therefore prepare for bloody war;
    These kegs must all be routed;
Or surely we despis'd shall be,
    And British courage doubted."

The royal band now ready stand,
    All rang'd in dread array, sir,
With stomach stout, to see it out,
    And make a bloody day, sir.
The cannons roar, from shore to shore,
    The small arms make a rattle:
Since wars began, I'm sure no man
    E'er saw so strange a battle.

The rebel dales, the rebel vales,
    With rebel trees surrounded,
The distant woods, the hills and floods,
    With rebel echoes sounded.
The fish below swam to and fro,
    Attack'd from every quarter:
Why sure, thought they, the devil's to pay,
    'Mongst folks above the water.

These kegs, 'tis said, though strongly made,
    Of rebel staves and hoops, sir,
Could not oppose their powerful foes,
    The conquering British troops, sir.
From morn till night, these men of might
    Display'd amazing courage;
And when the sun was fairly down,
    Retir'd to sup their porridge.

A hundred men with each a pen,
    Or more upon my word, sir,

It is most true, would be too few,
   Their valor to record, sir.
Such feats did they perform that day
   Upon those wicked kegs, sir,
That years to come, if they get home,
   They'll make their boasts and brags, sir.

With the spring of 1778 good news arrived from France. On May 2 Simeon Deane arrived in the royal frigate *Le Sensible* with the text of a treaty that had been concluded the previous February between France and the United States. The two countries agreed to make "common cause" in their struggle with Great Britain "and aid each other mutually with their good offices, their councils, and their forces . . . as becomes good and faithful allies."

The central purpose of this alliance, in French eyes, was "to maintain effectually the liberty, sovereignty, and independence, absolute and unlimited, of the said United States, as well in matters of government as of commerce." The French empire was locked in an age-old struggle with Great Britain; in one round of this contest, 1754–1763, France had lost its huge possessions in the New World—Canada and the Mississippi Valley. When news reached Paris in December 1777 of Burgoyne's defeat and the battle of Germantown, Louis XVI and his advisers began to view the colonists in a new light. Drawn into an alliance that guaranteed their independence and prevented a settlement with England, the Americans could help the French pay back old scores.

When news of the French alliance reached the American camp, there was great rejoicing; help from abroad in money, men, guns, and, above all, battleships, was seen at once as a decisive factor that could tip the scales of power against Britain and secure her defeat.

A celebration of the good news was held at Valley Forge on May 6. The men paraded in the morning; brigade chaplains read the text of the treaty, offered up prayers of thanksgiving, and delivered sermons. Then a grand parade took place, the troops marched and wheeled, and the guns were fired amid cheers for the king of France. "This *feu de joie*," wrote the *New York Journal*, "was conducted with great judgment and regularity. The gradual progression of the sound from the discharge of cannon and musketry, swelling and rebounding from the neighboring hills, and gently sweeping along the Schuyl-kill, with the intermingled huzzas . . . composed a military music more agreeable to a soldier's ear than the most finished pieces of your favorite Handel."

Afterwards Washington threw a party for the officers. The tables on which the refreshments stood were "shaded by elegant marquees, raised high, and arranged in a very striking and agreeable style. An excellent band of music attended during the entertainment . . . The wine circulated in the most genial manner—*To the King of France! the friendly European powers! the American States! the honorable Congress!*—and other toasts of similar nature, descriptive of the spirit of freemen."

In the Philadelphia camp, as we may imagine, the news was received with gloom. The loyalist *Pennsylvania Ledger* saw in the French alliance a big step toward the triumph of popery throughout Christendom and the consequent enslavement of mankind. "We do not only," lamented the *Ledger*, "run the manifest risk of becoming slaves ourselves . . . but we are doing everything in our power to overturn the Protestant religion, and extinguish every spark, both of civil and religious freedom, in the world!"

A more immediate danger to the Philadelphia loyalists was the imminent return of the revolutionaries. The threatened arrival of a French fleet meant that the British would lose naval superiority if they continued to divide their forces among the three bases at Rhode Island, New York, and Philadelphia. They had no choice but to evacuate the city and return to Manhattan.

But before they left, the British officers, like the Americans, had a party. The occasion was the resignation of Billy Howe as commander-in-chief; on May 18 Howe's subordinates gave him a gala farewell. The master of ceremonies was John Andre, who was determined that his show should far outstrip in splendor and luxuriance the miserable frolic at Valley Forge on May 6. "The fete," we are told,.

> began at 4 o'clock in the afternoon, by a grand procession on the Delaware, consisting of three divisions—a galley and ten flatboats in each division. In the center division was the Hussar galley, with the general, the admiral, General Sir Henry Clinton, and the ladies of their party. Three flatboats, with bands of music in each, led the procession.
>
> The flotilla proceeded to the Old Fort, where the officers and their ladies disembarked and walked, between two lines of grenadiers, to the tournament ground.

*British officers
dancing with Tory girls.
From a Pennsylvania Dutch pie plate.*

Here they were entertained by a medieval joust—officers on horseback, noncoms and privates dressed up as pages and squires. "The elegance and richness of the different dresses of the knights and squires, their horses' trappings and caparisons, the taste displayed in their mottoes and devices, the various evolutions and feats of arms they performed . . . surpassed the most sanguine expectations of the beholders." Then there was tea, dancing, and refreshments until 10:30 P.M., topped off, amid the oohs and aahs of the Tory girls (all dressed in gold, blue, and scarlet gowns, no less), with "a grand and beautiful display of fireworks."

After the fireworks "the company sat down to a supper consisting of a thousand and twenty-four dishes, in a magnificent apartment built for the occasion. . . . The herald of the *blended rose*, in his robes of ceremony, announced by sound of trumpet *the King's health; the Queen and the Royal Family, the Army and Navy,* and their respective commanders; *the Ladies.*"

But all good things come to an end. The British packed their bags, kissed the girls goodbye, and a month after the party they were gone. On June 18 the last troops were ferried across the Delaware at Gloucester Point to make the long trek back, across the Jersey flats, to New York. John Andre was sad as he rode along. His thoughts turned back to the happy winter days behind, especially the time he had spent in the company of a pretty seventeen-year-old, Peggy Shippen.

The Americans resumed occupation of Philadelphia as soon as the British had left; Benedict Arnold was appointed military commandant of the city. The rest of

Washington's forces scampered off in pursuit of the British. It was mid-June; the cherry trees had blossomed and were coming into fruit. "We passed through Princeton," wrote Joseph Martin,

and encamped in the open fields, the canopy of heaven for our tent. Early next morning we marched again, and came up with the rear of the British army. We followed them several days, arriving upon their camping ground within an hour after their departure from it. We had ample opportunity to see the devastation they had made in their rout; cattle killed and lying about the fields and pastures, some just in the position they were when shot down . . . household furniture hacked and broken to pieces; wells filled up and mechanics' and farmers' tools destroyed.

At Monmouth the Americans caught up with the British, and mauled them badly in an indecisive engagement fought on June 28 in the sweltering heat. The British and Hessians, in their heavy woolies, endured agonies. "Of the enemy's dead," wrote the *New York Journal*, "many have been found without wound, but being heavily clothed, they sank under the heat and fatigue." The patriots did not suffer in this way nearly as much as their antagonists, for, as Martin said, "on our march from Valley Forge through the Jersies, and at the boasted battle of Monmouth, a fourth part of our troops had not a scrap of anything but their ragged shirt flaps to cover their nakedness."

DARK DAY

Stalemate, 1778–1780

What great event, next will be sent
Upon this guilty land?
He only knows, who can dispose
All things at His command.

"A Few Lines Composed on the
Dark Day of May 19, 1780"

High hopes were set upon the French alliance; the
mood of the country in the spring of 1778 was one of
optimism and elation. "France" spelled troops and supplies, but principally sea power, a decisive factor in the
struggle that hitherto the Americans had lacked. In the
capital of Philadelphia, so recently reclaimed from the
British, gay preparations were made to receive the French
ambassador, M. Louis Gerard; he would be the first offi-
cial representative to the United States from a major
European state. The ceremonies took place on August 6,
1778; the *New York Journal* described them as follows:

In pursuance of the ceremonials established by Congress,
the Hon. Richard Henry Lee, Esquire, one of the Dele-

gates from Virginia, and the Hon. Samuel Adams, one of the Delegates from Massachusetts Bay, in a coach and six provided by Congress, waited upon the Minister at his house. In a few minutes the Minister and the two delegates entered the coach, Mr. Lee placing himself at the Minister's left hand on the back seat, Mr. Adams occupying the front seat.

Thus accompanied, M. Gerard proceeded at one o'clock to the State House, where Congress, seated in a wide semicircle, was waiting. The minister was led in; his secretary advanced and presented the ambassador's credentials to the president of Congress. Mr. Lee then formally introduced the minister to the gathering. "The President, the Congress, and the Minister," reported the *New York Journal,* "rose together: he bowed to the President and Congress, they bowed to him; whereupon the whole seated themselves. In a moment the Minister arose and made a speech to the Congress, they sitting . . . The President and the Congress then rose, and the President pronounced their answer to the speech, the Minister standing."

After further bowing on both sides, M. Gerard withdrew. Later in the day he was the guest of honor at a reception where many toasts were drunk in honor of the king of France and the American Revolution. "Thus," editorialized the *New York Journal,* "has a new and noble sight been exhibited in this new world—the representatives of the United States of America, solemnly giving public audience to a Minister Plenipotentiary from the most powerful prince in Europe."

The jubilation in Philadelphia was mingled with expectancy. The frigate that had brought M. Gerard to the capital was part of a French fleet, under the command of Vice Admiral Charles Hector, Comte d'Estaing, that had arrived in American waters in July and anchored off Sandy Hook. D'Estaing and Washington discussed a plan of attack. New York, England's main base for action against the United States, was the logical target for an assault; but the French ships were of deep draft and unable to cross the bar and enter the lower bay. D'Estaing and Washington therefore determined to make a joint attack on August 10, 1778, on the British position at Newport, Rhode Island.

Newport was a fine harbor located on the southwestern side of Rhode Island in Narragansett Bay; the British, as we have seen, originally occupied it in December 1776, at the end of their victorious New York campaign. Possession of Newport gave them many advantages. It was a base for a possible new invasion of New England, a center for the collection of supplies and forage for the British troops, and a naval station for shelter, refitting and provisioning.

One of the British officers at Newport at this time was our old friend Frederick Mackenzie, now promoted to captain, whom we last met during the New York campaign. Since coming to Newport at the end of 1776 he had been leading a pleasant existence there, engaged in the routine duties of an army of occupation, enlivened by frequent minor clashes with the American militia. "A fine sea breeze," noted Mackenzie complacently on July 7, 1777, "moderates the heat greatly, and makes this

Island a delightful residence during the extreme heats of the summer months."

One year later Mackenzie and his men were engaged in frantic preparations to defend Rhode Island against invasion by sea and by land in the event that the French fleet appeared. "Our whole attention," he wrote on July 21, 1778, "is now given to the increase of our means of defense in case of the appearance of the French fleet which it is generally expected will make an attempt on this Island very soon."

Washington's plan called for an invasion of Rhode Island by 10,000 Continental troops and militia under the command of Generals John Sullivan, Nathanael Greene, and John Hancock. French troops were to be landed on Conanicut Island and assault Newport from the west. The French navy would blockade the harbor and prevent British reinforcements and supplies from coming in. On July 29, while the militia were rapidly and enthusiastically assembling, the French fleet hove in view. "About 9 o'clock this morning," reported Mackenzie in his usual dry manner, "a fleet of large ships appeared to the south-east, standing for the harbor. They were very soon discovered to be French; and about 12 [noon] they came to off the south end of [Rhode] Island . . . They consist of 12 line of battleships and 4 frigates; with several small craft attending them." The following day, as French men o' war sailed up the ship channel, the British burned and sank their own vessels to avoid capture. "It was a most mortifying sight to us, who were spectators of this conflagration, to see so many fine frigates destroyed in so short a time, without any loss on the part of the enemy," Mackenzie wrote.

A few days later, on August 9, when French troops were already on Conanicut Island and Sullivan's forces had invaded Rhode Island from the northern end, the British mood changed to one of joy. A fleet of thirty-five sail was sighted in Long Island Sound! "It soon became certain," wrote Mackenzie, "that the fleet in sight was that under the command of Lord [Richard] Howe from New York . . . the spirits of the whole garrison were at this period elevated to the highest pitch."

The fresh wind from the southwest that was bearing Howe under full sail toward Newport boded no good for the French—if the admiral could enter the harbor before nightfall he would have the French fleet trapped and at his mercy. But the wind dropped and the weather changed. On August 10 the wind began to blow from the northwest, and it was now D'Estaing who crowded sail and moved out of Narragansett Bay in full force to challenge the British, who had anchored out in the sound, seven miles to the southwest. On August 11 the wind veered to the northeast; by the next day, amid drenching rain, it had risen to hurricane force. Both fleets were scattered, and suffered damage. Howe made his way back to New York to refit.

On Rhode Island the tents of the troops were torn to shreds by the storm, but Sullivan, nothing daunted, continued his advance southward down the island and laid siege to Newport. On August 19 the French fleet was sighted again, off Block Island. What followed was reported in the *New York Gazette*:

The French fleet returned to Rhode Island on Thursday last [August 20] but had suffered so considerably in the late storm . . . that they judged it necessary to retire in order to refit; in consequence of which resolution, the whole fleet sailed for Boston yesterday [August 22]. General Sullivan, with the other general officers, were of opinion that they had not suffered to such a degree but that they were capable of sufficiently cooperating with the Americans in the reduction of Newport, without danger to the fleet; consequently the general, in the name of all the general officers of his army, protested against the count's withdrawing with his fleet and army at this critical juncture, as this expedition would not have been undertaken at this time, had it not been for the assurance he had given of assisting the American army to the utmost of his power.

D'Estaing's refusal to listen to these pleas sealed the fate of the campaign. Many of the militia were enlisted for twenty days, and these men were now going home. During the night of August 28 Sullivan struck camp, and his forces marched away; all of Rhode Island was free of American troops by September 1. The American forces had retired not a second too soon. That very day Sir Henry Clinton sailed into Narragansett Bay with a fleet of seventy sail and eight regiments of troops. But for contrary winds that delayed the British reinforcements, the Americans, abandoned by their French allies, would have found themselves in the same kind of trap that faced Washington on Long Island in 1776.

As for the American Tories, they did not fail to gloat

over the collapse of Franco-American cooperation and the total discomfiture of their foes. As a matter of fact, they hugged each other in glee and laughed till the tears ran down their faces. Witness a witty song published in *Rivington's Gazette* on October 3, 1778:

Yankee Doodle's Expedition to Rhode Island
TUNE: YANKEE DOODLE

From Louis, Monsieur Gerard came
To Congress in this town, sir,
They bowed to him, and he to them,
And then they all sat down, sir.
"Begar," said Monsieur, "one grand coup
You shall bientôt *behold, sir,"*
This was believed as gospel true,
And Jonathan felt bold, sir.

So Yankee Doodle did forget
The sound of British drum, sir,
How oft it made him quake and sweat
In spite of Yankee rum, sir.
He took his wallet on his back
His rifle on his shoulder,
And vowed Rhode Island to attack
Before he was much older.

In dread array their tattered crew
Advanced with colors spread, sir,
Their fifes played Yankee-doodle-doo,
King Hancock at their head, sir.

What numbers bravely crossed the seas,
 I cannot well determine,
A swarm of rebels and of fleas
 And every other vermin.

As Jonathan so much desired
 To shine in martial glory,
D'Estaing with politesse retired
 To leave him all the glory.
He left him what was better yet,
 At least it was more use, sir,
He left him for a quick retreat
 A very good excuse, sir.

To stay unless he ruled the sea,
 He thought would not be right, sir,
And Continental troops, said he,
 On islands should not fight, sir.
Another cause with these combined
 To throw him in the dumps, sir,
For Clinton's name alarmed his mind,
 And made him stir his stumps, sir.

Thus the bright promise of the spring of 1778 was
not borne out: the colonial cause faced its darkest hour,
for stalemate had set in. The British were powerless to
occupy American soil and subdue the nation; the patriots
were too weak in strength and too poor in resources to
conquer the British. Soldiers fought, and were not paid,
starved, or even lay abed to cover their nakedness while
others grew fat on the profits of war. To add to the hard-

ship of the people, inflation had set in and the Continental currency was close to worthless.

The horror of this stalemate—the bulldog's fangs in the side of the boar, powerless to kill and unable to let go—was underlined in 1778 and the following years by incessant raids upon coastal towns and frontier settlements. The British, of course, had been conducting raids for plunder, cattle, and forage since the beginning of the war, but now the raids grew in intensity and frequency, spreading panic throughout British America from Georgia to Maine. They signified the development of a new technique to terrorize the people and reduce them to submission, using vengeful loyalists and loot-hungry Indians for the purpose. " 'Tis surprising," commented Captain Mackenzie in September, "what an effect the burning of houses, and destroying their property, has had upon the Rebels. *'Tis now become evident, that this way of carrying on the war, is the only effectual method of bringing them to a sense of their duty.*" [Emphasis added.]

Typical of this new tactic of systematic savagery was the descent of Colonel John Butler on Cherry Valley, New York. Butler was a loyalist from Connecticut who headed a band of Tories and Indians. He first gained notoriety in July 1778 by attacking the frontier settlement of Wyoming Valley in Pennsylvania—burning houses, barns, and crops, killing the cattle and massacring the inhabitants. Thereafter Butler extended his operations to the back country of New Jersey, and on November 11, 1778, descended upon the outlying settlement of Cherry Valley and laid it waste with fire and sword. An American officer at the scene described the invading force as "800 in number, consisting of 500 Indians, commanded by Joseph Brant, 50 Regulars under Captain Colvill, and another captain with some of Johnson's Rangers, and above 200 Tories." The raiders first attempted to take the local stronghold, Fort Alden. The fort, defended by a regiment of Continental troops, put up a good resistance and fought the raiders off. Butler and his men then turned their full fury on the people of the community. "The next day," the officer wrote,

they made it their whole business to collect horses, cattle, and sheep, which they effected, and at sunset left the place. The enemy killed, scalped, and most barbarously murdered, thirty-two inhabitants, chiefly women and children . . . They burnt twenty-four houses with all the grain, etc., and took above sixty inhabitants prisoners, part of whom they released on going off. They committed the most inhuman barbarities on most of the dead. Robert Henderson's head was cut off, his skull bone was cut out with the scalp. Mr. Willis' sister was ripped up, a child of Mr. Willis', two months old, scalped, and an arm cut off, and many others as cruelly treated. Many of the inhabitants and soldiers shut out from the fort, lay all night in the rain with the children, who suffered very much. The cattle that were not easy to drive, they shot. We were informed by the prisoners they sent back, that the lieutenant colonel, all the officers and Continental soldiers, were stripped and drove naked before them.

The same month, at the far end of the country, 500 Tories made a raid on Sunbury, Georgia, driving off 1,000 head of cattle, 200 horses, and a number of slaves, and

American farmer, Peter Francisco,
attacking British soldiers outside an inn in Virginia.

burning all the houses in their path. Another and even more ambitious raid was conducted against New Haven and Fairfield, Connecticut, in July 1779. On July 4 transports landed more than 2,000 men, many of whom were Hessians, who then engaged in an orgy of looting and destruction. The *New York Journal* reported:

They vented their fury upon the persons and effects of all who unfortunately fell under their power. They plundered the houses of everything they could carry away or convert to their own use, and broke or destroyed every whole article of household goods and furniture. . . . The few men who stayed in town, most of whom were old, infirm, or Tories, were treated with the greatest abuse and insolent ferocity—stripped and plundered of everything valuable about them, and on the slightest pretenses, or even without any pretense at all, inhumanly stabbed with bayonets, shot, or otherwise murdered. . . . [At New Haven] few, if any, of the young women . . . nor not all the old, or even the Negroes, escaped violation —some in the presence of their husbands, and others by great numbers successively.

Another story, published in *Rivington's Gazette*, denied that rape was committed at Fairfield, but charged that the soldiery "robbed women of buckles, rings, bonnets, aprons, and handkerchiefs; they abused them with the foulest and most profane language, threatened their lives, presenting bayonets to their breasts."

British writers denied these charges, saying that they were malicious inventions or that, if they were true, the Americans were to blame since they had brought the war upon themselves by their stubborn and wrong-headed resistance. Congress, wrote the *New York Gazette* on August 16, 1779, was "justly chargeable before God and the world, with all the calamities which America now suffers, and with all those other and greater calamities which it will probably hereafter suffer in the course of this unnatural contest." A British officer, writing in June 1780, pointed out that since the entire population appeared to be involved in the war, the British army was justified in a policy of "frightfulness" directed at soldiers and civilians alike. "The soldiers," he said,

received with smiles one moment, and the following instant butchered (for in a military view it merits no other name) by a set of people who, by their clothing and appointments, cannot be distinguished from the quiet inhabitants of the country, may well be supposed to be exasperated; nor need we be surprised at their using the torch to dwellings which they find hourly occupied by armed men, who either want the generosity or the spirit to close the present unhappy contest by a manly, open, soldier-like decorum.

The winter of 1779–1780 was the coldest in living memory, colder even than the winter of Valley Forge. Washington's ragged troops lay in snowbound encampments in New Jersey and the New York highlands. There were many cases of frostbite, and some men froze to death at their posts or in the drifts. Joseph Martin, at the Baskenridge camp, recalled: "We were absolutely starved. I do solemnly declare that I did not put a single morsel of victuals into my mouth for four days and as many nights, except a little bit of birch bark I gnawed off a stick of wood." This, as the *Maryland Gazette* pointed out, happened because "by the severity of the weather, and drifting of the snow . . . the roads were rendered impassable, and all supplies of provisions cut off."

Civilians, too, suffered severely. At Fishkill, New York, it was reported that "several ships and many lives have been lost by the monstrous bodies of ice floating in our bay," and at Rhinebeck "a Negro man, with a sleigh and two horses, the property of Mrs. Montgomery, were lost by falling through the ice." At Boston, on December 28, "a wagoner, his horses, and four oxen were found frozen to death near the dyke, on Boston neck."

The complete freezing over of Long Island Sound and the lower Hudson made easier British raids across the ice against communities in New Jersey and Westchester. In the middle of January 1780, 400 men under Colonel Van Buskirk

crossed on the ice from Staten Island to Trembly's Point, about three miles from Elizabethtown . . . set fire to the Presbyterian meeting and court house, which were consumed; plundered, insulted, and took off some of the inhabitants, and retreated. . . . The same night another party of the enemy . . . passed over the North River in sleighs, to Powle's Hook; from thence through Bergen, the nearest way to Newark. They then set fire to the academy, which was consumed, during which time a party was detached to several of the inhabitants' houses, which they rifled of the most valuable effects; that which was not portable they destroyed. They took off Justice Hedden and Robert Neil, Jr., two of the inhabitants. The former gentleman was taken out of his bed, and without any of his clothes on except his shirt and a pair of stockings—carried off, notwithstanding the strongest solicitations of Mrs. Hedden to the officers, for permission for her husband to dress himself. She received two wounds with a bayonet, one in the face, the other in the breast. . . . A few militia being hastily collected, pursued their rear, by which means five of the enemy fell into their hands. Two of them died a short time after from the intense cold. Justice Hedden is so frost-bitten, that it is thought he will lose both his legs.

Spring found the British, not the Americans, with the initiative. Sir Henry Clinton returned to Charleston, South Carolina, to secure a base for a planned invasion of the South, and to settle an old score. In April 1780 the general, with ten men o' war, ran before the guns of Fort Moultrie in a high wind, laid siege to the town, and took it on May 12 after a combined assault by land and sea. It was a major disaster for the American cause; the British gained a first-class port and took 4,500 prisoners into the bargain. Sir Henry then sailed back to New York, leaving his second-in-command, Lord Cornwallis, to complete what he had begun, the subjugation of the South.

On May 19, one week after this catastrophe, a great darkness spread over New England. "As early as ten in the morning," wrote *Viator* in the *Boston Country Journal* of "the dark day," May 19:

*a thick darkness came over the face of the country, so
that it was impossible to move about the house without
the assistance of a candle. . . . In the time of the greatest darkness, some of the dunghill fowls went to their
roost; cocks crowed in answer to each other, as they commonly do in the night; wood-cocks, which are night birds,
whistled as they do only in the dark; frogs peeped; in
short there was the appearance of midnight at noonday.*

Some people considered the darkness a sign of God's
judgment and impending doom; others attributed it to
smog, caused by smoke from huge fires where the forest
had been burning for several days.

In August 1780 George Washington appointed Benedict Arnold commandant of West Point. Arnold, who
had been for many months in secret communication with
the British, hastened his plans to turn the fortress over
to the enemy.

West Point is situated in the New York highlands at
a point where the Hudson River passes in a narrow channel between steep banks and mountain ridges. After the
campaign against Burgoyne in 1777 Washington became
aware of the strategic importance of this place, and proceeded to fortify it. By 1780 there was good reason for
both sides to believe that whoever held this bastion also
held the keys to the American future. With West Point
in American hands, no British men o' war could sail
through the channel. But if the British seized West Point
they could navigate the river as far as Albany, and thus
control the entire length of the Hudson to that point.
Sealing off communication between the New England

and central states would then be a simple matter. If this were done, the revolutionary cause might either be defeated or its triumph indefinitely postponed.

The man who now planned treason was a brave field commander who had many times shown his readiness to die for the revolutionary cause. In 1775 he disputed with Ethan Allen for the honor of capturing Ticonderoga; in the fall of that year he organized and led the force that invaded Canada across the wilds of Maine. On January 1, 1776, he led the assault on Quebec in a freezing blizzard. He performed great services for the patriot cause in the Hudson Valley in 1777. His native Connecticut had reason to be grateful to him that year, for driving British raiders from Norwalk and Danbury.

In 1778, when the Americans retook Philadelphia, Arnold became military commandant of the city. He courted Peggy Shippen, the girl John Andre had left behind so reluctantly, and married her in 1779. To provide luxuries for Peggy and himself, he fell into debt, entered dubious speculations, and was reprimanded by Washington. This was the man who now lost faith that the American revolutionaries could prevail against the mightiest empire in the world.

On the night of September 21 Arnold met with John Andre in a forest of firs on the west bank of the Hudson above Haverstraw to negotiate the surrender. When the meeting was over the ship that had brought Andre upriver—the *Vulture*—had gone, fleeing south again in the face of American fire from the shore. So Andre made his way back to New York City by land, in civilian clothes. On September 24 three militiamen—John Paulding, Isaac van Wert, and David Williams—stopped him at Tarrytown, searched him, and found a map of West Point hidden in his boot. When the news came to Arnold, he fled downriver. Andre was taken to American headquarters at Tappan, New Jersey, tried and sentenced to death as a spy.

On October 2 the army and a huge crowd of civilians assembled in a field on Tappan Hill to witness the execution. A soldier described the scene:

A kind of procession was formed, by placing a guard in single file on each side of the road. In front were a large number of American officers of high rank, on horseback. These were followed by the wagon with coffin; then a large number of officers on foot, with Andre in their midst. The procession moved slowly up a hill . . . to an open field in which was a very high gallows, made of two poles and crosspiece.

When the procession came to the place of execution, Andre waited while the cart, with its black coffin, was drawn under the gallows. He put his foot on a stone, rolled it, and fought a choking sensation in his throat. Then, when the wagon was ready, the young man stepped up onto it, took off his hat, and surveyed the scene. "He was dressed," wrote the soldier,

in what I should call a complete British uniform; coat of the brightest scarlet, faced or trimmed with the most beautiful green. His vest and britches were of bright buff, very similar to those of military officers in Connecticut today. He had a long and beautiful head of hair, which,

Execution scene from songsheet
"The Death of Major Andre."

*agreeably to the fashion, was wound with a black ribbon
and hung down his back.*

While the crowd watched in silence, Andre loosened
the kerchief at his neck, unfastened his collar, and ban-
daged his eyes. And now the audience of Americans was
in tears: an innocent man was here compelled to die for
another's crime. Then the wagon was pulled away; the
body swung, and was still. "He remained hanging," wrote
the soldier,

*twenty or thirty minutes, and during that time the cham-
bers of death were never stiller than the multitude by
which he was surrounded. Orders were given to cut the
rope and take him down, without letting him fall; this
was done, and his body laid carefully on the ground.*

Then the black coffin with the body of John Andre
was laid to rest on Tappan Hill. Years later the remains
were taken back to Westminster Abbey, in London. But
there is a marker at the spot that reads: "His death
though according to the stern code of war, moved even
his enemies to pity; and both armies mourned the fate of
one so young and brave."

Ballad of Major Andre

He with a scouting party went down to Tarrytown,
Where they met a British officer, a man of high renown;
Who said unto these gentlemen, "You're of the British cheer,
I trust that you can tell me if there is danger near?"

Then up spoke this young hero, John Paulding was his name;
"Oh tell us where you're going, sir, and also whence you came?"
"I bear the British flag, sir, I've a pass to go this way,
I'm on an expedition, I have no time to stay."

Then round him came this company, and bade him to dismount;
"Come, tell us where you're going, give us a strict account;
For now we are resolved, that you shall ne'er pass by."
On a strict examination they found he was a spy!

He begged for his liberty, he pled for his discharge,
And oftentimes he told them, if they'd set him at large,
"Here's all the gold and silver, I have laid up in store,
And when I reach the city I will send you ten times more."

"We scorn your gold and silver, you have laid up in store,
And when you reach the city, you need not send us more."
He saw that his conspiracy would soon be brought to light,
He begg'd for pen and paper, and asked for to write.

The story came to Arnold, commanding at the Fort:
He called for the *Vulture*, and sailed for New York;
Now Arnold to New York has gone, a-fighting for his King,
And left poor Major Andre on the gallows for to swing.

Andre was executed, he look'd both meek and mild;
Around on the spectators most pleasantly he smiled;
It moved each eye to pity, and every heart there bled,
And everyone wished him releas'd, and Arnold in his stead.

He was a man of honor, in Britain he was born,
To die upon the gallows most highly he did scorn:
And now his life has reached its end, so young and blooming still,
In Tappan's quiet countryside he sleeps upon the hill.

☆ | *12* | ☆

THE BONNY BUNCH OF ROSES
Cornwallis and the Southern Campaign, 1780–1781

And I never will return again
Till I have conquered the Bonny Bunch of Roses O!
English folk song, "The Bonny Bunch of Roses O"

During the year May 1780 to April 1781 when Clinton and Cornwallis were attempting to conquer the Carolinas, interesting things were happening in Rhode Island. On July 11, 1780, a French expeditionary force arrived at Newport, and stayed there for nearly a year, waiting for a chance to participate in the Revolution. The commander of this force was the Marquis de Rochambeau; his soldiers were organized in four regiments—Bourbonnais, Deux-Ponts, Soissonnais, and Saintonge. All were outfitted in beautiful regimental uniforms that caused a sensation wherever they were seen. The Soissonnais were especially dazzling: their coats had rose-colored lapels and facings, their caps were decorated with a big rosette and a snowy plume.

General Rochambeau's aide-de-camp was a young officer from the Rhineland, Baron Ludwig von Closen. Closen,

Canadian Indians visiting Newport, Rhode Island,
sketched by Baron Ludwig von Closen in 1781.

a captain in the Deux-Ponts regiment, was fascinated by America and its people; he put together a careful journal of his observations and experiences while in this country. The original manuscript perished in a fire; only a handwritten transcript in the Library of Congress survived. Recently translated and published by an American scholar, the Closen *Journal* is now an important source for the study of the last phase of the revolutionary war.

Closen began to explore Rhode Island as soon as he came ashore; notwithstanding the waste and destruction that war had inflicted, he found the place delightful:

This island is, at its greatest extent, almost fifteen miles long and five wide. This must have been a very pleasant country before the war, since, despite its disasters, such as the destruction of many houses and of all the woods, this island still affords a charming place for a sojourn. All the fields of the different proprietors are enclosed by walls of stones, heaped one on top of the other, or by wooden barriers called fences, which make for a pleasing variety. The soil is very good, rich without being too heavy.

The young aristocrat enjoyed a pleasant social life at Newport. Used to the formality of European society, he was amused at the free and easy American manners.

You lean on your neighbors without ceremony, you put your elbows on the table during dinner. . . . The outward appearance of Americans rather generally indicates

carelessness, and almost thoughtlessness; but it is aston-
ishing that with this apparent indifference they fight with
so much bravery. . . . Who may believe that an Ameri-
can who scarcely dares go out of his house on a rainy day,
the moment he has a musket on his shoulder, braves every
danger and the most difficult weather? You cannot find
a man of 30 years who has not borne arms.

Closen not only liked the Americans but found their
food much to his taste: buttered toast, ham or smoked
fish for breakfast; roast beef, puddings and pies for
dinner. It did distress him, though, that nowhere, even
among the well-to-do, were table napkins provided.
Everyone, he marveled, wiped their faces on the table-
cloth.

While the French waited patiently on Rhode Island
—usually a British fleet was hovering offshore, to see
that they didn't go anyplace by sea—great events were developing in the South. Less than a year of campaigning
in the Carolinas convinced Cornwallis that the conquest
of that province with its huge distances and its teeming
guerrilla bands was impossible.

In this southern campaign Cornwallis, evidently, had
learned little from the British experience in New Jersey
in 1777. The occupiers behaved with the same stupid
brutality as before, and suffered the same consequences.
Patriot bands sprang up to cut supply lines, to harry and
annihilate British detachments. The backwoods folk rallied around leaders like Francis Marion, Thomas Sumter,
and Andrew Pickens in battles of unexampled bitterness
against the invader and his loyalist allies.

Not only were there guerrillas everywhere to contend with, but Washington's southern army had a new and able commander, General Nathanael Greene. A Rhode Islander, Greene was born at Warwick on the west side of Narragansett Bay, in the very same village to which the British general, Prescott, had been taken after his capture by William Barton in July 1777. Greene, who had been with Washington at the siege of Boston and at the crossing of the Delaware on Christmas Day in 1776, took command of the southern Continental forces in December 1780. In the year of campaigning that followed he scored brilliant successes over the British. Much credit goes to him for organizing and leading the effort that secured the total collapse of Britain's southern strategy in the year 1781.

In order to "pacify" the South, Cornwallis had to seek out and destroy the Continental forces and militia that rallied around them. The British general had made a good start when he met Johnny Gates at Camden on August 16, 1780, and inflicted a crushing defeat. Cornwallis then discovered what other British generals had already found out: even when you beat the Americans, it didn't seem to make much difference.

When you won a battle, exactly what did you win? The defeated enemy melted away; the guerrillas resumed their attacks on your supply line; you had to withdraw to the security of a fortified post or coastal base. Then the enemy resumed control of the territory which you had won at such a cost.

Faced with this kind of opposition, Cornwallis asked himself, Why not move north to Virginia? It was a wealthy state, and could provide food and forage for men and horses; other British generals, including Benedict Arnold, were operating there. Why not concentrate forces, cooperate, and conquer Virginia?

To Virginia, accordingly, by a long overland march at the end of April, Cornwallis went. Sir Henry Clinton was far from approving this change in his subordinate's plans; but eventually he directed Cornwallis to secure Yorktown, on the York River, as a suitable base for operations. This was done on August 4, 1781.

While Cornwallis was moving northward to Virginia in May 1781, Washington and Rochambeau were discussing their plan of action. Rochambeau urged an attack on the British forces in Virginia, but Washington felt strongly that the best thing to do was to storm the main enemy base—New York. Rochambeau deferred to the commander-in-chief. The French troops left Rhode Island early in June to join the American forces at White Plains. Closen and his young officer friends were enchanted at this turn of events. They could look forward not only to fighting the British, but to other pleasures: "seeing new lands, making new acquaintances, and becoming familiar with the other provinces."

And so the French started off, marching westward from Providence amid the gray stone walls and the flowering shrubs of a flaming New England spring. The march through central Connecticut took a little more than two weeks, being slowed by heat, bad roads, and the high hills of the Taconic range. Closen went on ahead of the Deux-Ponts and reached White Plains on

July 4; there he got his first glimpse of the American army. "It was really painful to see these brave men," he wrote, "almost naked, with only some trousers and little linen jackets; most of them without stockings, but, believe it or not, very cheerful and healthy in appearance. A quarter of them were Negroes, merry, confident, and sturdy."

Late in July Washington and Rochambeau probed the defenses of Manhattan. An attack was unthinkable: Clinton was well entrenched and had a large army, and further reinforcements were on their way. Then, on August 14, heartening news arrived from Newport. Admiral de Grasse, who commanded the main French fleet in the West Indies, was ready for operations against the British in American waters; at the very moment that Washington read his dispatch, de Grasse was actually on his way to Chesapeake Bay with thirty-four ships of the line and 3,000 soldiers. Scarcely had this information arrived when it was followed by a letter from the Marquis de Lafayette in Virginia: Cornwallis' army had settled in at Yorktown.

It was now Washington's turn to give in to Rochambeau. The decision was made to move the armies as rapidly and secretly as possible to Yorktown. This was a military gamble, made on the chance that Cornwallis would stay put long enough to get caught and that de Grasse would indeed show up like he said he would. If both these things happened, the British army would be caught in a trap between the French fleet by sea and the besieging forces by land.

On August 19 the French and American troops left

New York and moved into New Jersey. Rumors were spread industriously that an attack on New York was imminent. Rochambeau went so far as to give orders for the building of bread ovens at Chatham, New Jersey, "in order to make Clinton believe that we were seriously considering an attack on New York, and that the army would remain encamped in that region." That he did succeed in fooling Clinton there is little doubt. But Captain Frederick Mackenzie had a much cannier estimate of the situation. His opinion, which he confided to his *Diary* on August 29, was that

the scheme of the enemy has all along been to make their effort against the army in Virginia under Lord Cornwallis. To this end they have made all possible show of attacking New York, and moved down twice with greatest part of their force to our advanced posts, to induce the commander-in-chief to withdraw part of the troops from Virginia. . . . The French frigate that lately arrived from the West Indies [i.e., with the dispatch from de Grasse], probably brought certain information of the time of their fleet sailing from that part of the world, in consequence of which the rebel army moved to pass the Hudson, and the French squadron took the first opportunity of leaving Newport, to meet de Grasse in a certain latitude, and then to occupy the Chesapeake; by which they will secure the movement of the rebel army to form a junction with Lafayette and make an attack on Cornwallis, and prevent our sending reinforcements to him. Thus by threatening us with a siege, the enemy have been suffered . . . to pass the Hudson and to advance a good way into New Jersey without molestation or obstruction.

The only thing that the British could do to prevent the looming disaster, Mackenzie concluded, was "to move with all our force into New Jersey, so as to keep close to Mr. Washington, and prevent him from moving southwards." Mackenzie, of course, was absolutely right; but then, he was only a captain, not a commander-in-chief.

Once the patriot forces were well on their way, Closen, who knew from the start what had been planned, revealed the truth to his fellow officer, the Vicomte des Deux-Ponts, under an oath of the strictest secrecy. One can imagine the impression that the news made upon the vicomte; the sharing of such confidences, Closen wrote complacently, "could only strengthen our friendship."

At the end of August the troops reached Philadelphia; here General Rochambeau decided to take a trip down the Delaware by boat so that he might view the famous fortifications (Mud Island, Red Bank, Billingsport) where Joseph Martin and his friends had made so gallant a stand in November 1777. They sailed by these ruins on September 5; and were refreshing themselves with bread, butter, and tea, when

We discerned in the distance General Washington, standing on the shore and waving his hat and a white handkerchief joyfully. There was good reason for this; for he informed us as we disembarked that M. de Grasse had arrived in Chesapeake Bay with 28 ships of the line

and 3,000 troops, whom he had already landed so that they might join M. de Lafayette, in order to prevent Cornwallis from escaping by land, while he [de Grasse] would block his egress by sea. The entire army shared our generals' joy in having their calculations work out so well.

Closen shared the opinion of the soldiers that Cornwallis would be taken soon. Had he known what was happening in Virginia on that very day, September 5, he might not have been so positive in his prediction. That day Admiral Graves put in an appearance in Chesapeake Bay with his entire fleet in order to block the French squadron, under Admiral Barras, which had come down with men and munitions from Rhode Island. We can imagine Graves's surprise when he found that he had run into de Grasse himself. The decisive naval encounter of the war was at hand; if de Grasse was beaten or turned tail now, hopes for victory over the British would be indefinitely postponed.

The two fleets exchanged broadsides and then maneuvered for a number of days. The British suffered more damage than the French, both from gunfire and windstorm. Graves was reluctant in this condition to challenge de Grasse's superior force, and the equinoctial gales were coming on. He sailed off to New York to find shelter and to refit. Mastery of the sea off the Virginia coast remained with the French.

The ominous significance of British failure to break the French fleet's control of the Virginia waters was not lost on Captain Mackenzie. On September 13, as

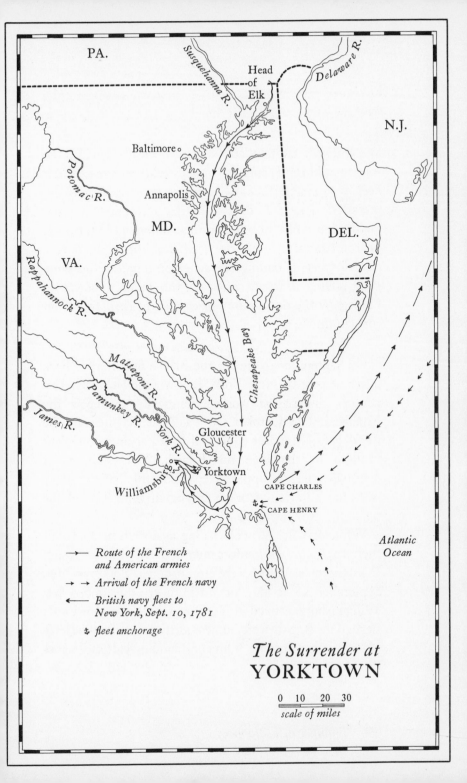

PA.

Susquehanna R.

Head
of
Elk

Delaware R.

N.J.

Baltimore

Potomac R.

Annapolis

MD.

DEL.

VA.

Rappahannock R.

Mattaponi R.

Pamunkey R.

York R.

James R.

Chesapeake Bay

Gloucester

Yorktown

Williamsburg

CAPE CHARLES

CAPE HENRY

Atlantic
Ocean

→ Route of the French
and American armies

→ → Arrival of the French navy

← British navy flees to
New York, Sept. 10, 1781

⚓ fleet anchorage

The Surrender at
YORKTOWN

0 10 20 30
scale of miles

he waited anxiously for news of the naval encounter, he wrote:

We certainly are now at the most critical period of the war. Should the French gain such an advantage over our fleet as to enable them to continue their operations un-molested against Lord Cornwallis, our hopes in that quarter rest entirely on the firmness of him and his troops; on the contrary should our fleet beat theirs, we have a fair prospect of ending the rebellion, and, at the same time, giving a severe blow to the military power of France, by the destruction, or capture of their troops on this continent.

On September 19 and 20 the British fleet limped back into the port of New York. In the following days car-penters and riggers worked frantically to repair the damage; but by October 1 it was clear that it would be weeks before the fleet could put to sea again in sufficient strength to challenge the French. Mackenzie noted dejectedly that "it appears very doubtful that the Navy will after all attempt or undertake anything toward the relief of Lord Cornwallis."

While the British were racing against time to repair their ships, embark reinforcements, and put to sea again, Washington's armies were approaching Yorktown. On September 28, a day of torrid heat, the troops left Williamsburg, arrived at Yorktown, and placed it under siege. The British were subjected to an artillery barrage of harrowing intensity. "Our commanding battery," wrote Private Martin, was on the near bank of the river and contained ten heavy guns; the next was a bomb battery of three large mortars; and so on through the whole line. The whole number, American and French, was ninety-two cannon, mortars and howitzers. . . . All were upon the tip-toe of expectation and impatience to see the signal given to open the whole line of batteries, which was to be the hoisting of the American flag in the ten-gun battery. About noon the much wished-for signal went up. I confess I felt a secret pride swell my heart when I saw the star-spangled banner waving majestically in the very faces of our implacable adversaries. . . . The siege was carried on warmly for several days, when most of the guns in the enemy's works were silenced.

As days went by, the siege lines closed in and the enemy's outlying fortifications were stormed and captured. On October 17 Cornwallis, who had waited in vain for help from New York, gave in. His batteries had been demolished by enemy fire, food was almost gone, and sickness raging. On October 19 the British army marched out and formally surrendered. An American military surgeon, James Thacher, recorded the scene:

At about 12 o'clock, the combined army was arranged and drawn up in two lines extending more than a mile in length. The Americans were drawn up in a line on the right side of the road, and the French occupied the left. At the head of the former the great American commander, mounted on his noble courser, took his station, attended by his aides. At the head of the latter was posted the excellent Count Rochambeau and his suite. The

Washington and Lafayette at Yorktown,
by Reuben Law Reed, about 1860.

French troops, in complete uniform, displayed a martial and noble appearance, their band of music, of which the timbrel formed a part, is a delightful novelty, and produced while marching to the ground a most enchanting effect. The Americans though not all in uniform nor their dress so neat, yet exhibited an erect soldierly air, and every countenance beamed with satisfaction and joy. The concourse of spectators from the country was prodigious, in point of numbers probably equal to the military, but universal silence and order prevailed.

Lord Cornwallis refused to attend the surrender ceremonies, for he found the ordeal too humiliating; his troops were led out from Yorktown by General O'Hara. "This officer," Thacher tells us, "was followed by the conquered troops in a slow and solemn step, with shouldered arms, colors cased and drums beating a British march." The army was conducted to a field to stack their arms. Here, says Thacher, "the spirit and pride of the British soldier was put to the severest test, here their mortification could not be concealed . . . many of the soldiers manifested a sullen temper, throwing their arms on the pile with violence, as if determined to render them useless."

Lord Cornwallis' Surrender

Voice

(Guitar Instrumental)

Come all ye brave A - mer - i - cans, The _ truth to you _ I'll _ tell, 'Tis

The Bonny Bunch of Roses 273

sum - moned_Lord Corn - wal - lis To _

fight or else_ give_ o'er.

The summons then to be served
        Was sent unto my Lord,
Which made him feel like poor Burgoyne,
        And quickly draw his sword.
Say, must I give these glittering troops,
        These ships and Hessians too,
And yield to Gen'ral Washington
        And his bold rebel crew?

A grand council then was called,
        His Lordship gave command,
Say, what think you now, my heroes,
        To yield you may depend—
For don't you see the bomb shells fly,
        And cannons loud do roar,
Count de Grasse lies in the harbor,
        And Washington's on shore.

'Twas the nineteenth of October,
     In the year eighty-one,
Lord Cornwallis he surrender'd
     To General Washington:
They marched from their posts, brave boys,
     And quickly grounded arms,
Rejoice, ye brave Americans,
     With music's sweetest charms.

Six thousand chosen British troops
     To Washington resign'd,
Besides some ships and Hessians,
     That could not stay behind;
With refugees and blackamores;
     O what a direful crew!
It was then he had some thousands,
     But now he's got but few.

My Lord has gone unto New York,
     Sir Harry for to see;
For to send home this dreadful news
     Unto His Majesty;
To contradict some former lines,
     That once to him was sent,
That he and his bold British troops,
     They conquer'd where they went.

Here's a health to great Washington,
     And his brave army too,
And likewise to our worthy Greene,
     To him much honor's due.
May we subdue those English troops,
     And clear the eastern shore,
That we may live in peace, my boys,
     Whilst wars they are no more.

A *fine portrait of*
an American black man,
by John Singleton Copley (1738-1815).

The next day Closen accompanied Rochambeau to Yorktown to call upon Lord Cornwallis. "I will never forget," he wrote,

how frightful and disturbing was the appearance of the city of York, from the fortifications on the crest to the strand below. One could not take three steps without running into some great holes made by bombs, some splinters, some balls, some half-covered trenches, with scattered white or Negro arms or legs, and some bits of uniform. Most of the houses were riddled by cannon fire.

Numbers of black slaves took part in the siege. Many more, some of them sick and dying, were turned loose by Cornwallis when he could no longer use or feed them. "They might be seen," wrote Joseph Martin, "scattered about in every direction, dead and dying, with pieces of burnt Indian corn in their hands and mouth, even of those that were dead."

CONCLUSION

The Revolution ought not to pass into history as an event without meaning.

François-Noël Babeuf, "Defense Before
the High Court of Vendôme"

At first sight it seems strange that the American people were victorious in their struggle with the British: the balance of military power was so obviously against them. Britain possessed a professional army formidable both in numbers and discipline, well armed, well clothed, and well supplied. The officers were well trained in the arts and sciences of war, and devoted their lives to the practice of their profession. The navy that convoyed these troops and their baggage to the New World was second to none in numerical size, fire power, and fighting tradition. It could transport troops at will to any part of the American coast, land them, and supply them indefinitely. It could also subject the coastal towns and cities to any punishment by artillery bombardment that it chose to inflict. The entire war-making machine was sustained by a well-developed manufacturing system that wove its clothes, forged its guns, and manned the yards where the wooden ships were made.

The American revolutionaries, by contrast, had no army and no officer corps; they had to build their military organization from scratch. Absence of the most fundamental necessities—ammunition, food, and equipment —often presented the question whether they would be able to stay in the field at all. To fight their battles the revolutionaries frequently had to rely on raw militia, men with rudimentary military training who had good reason to fly terror-stricken at the sight of the pitiless, methodical, bayonet-toting, red-coated killers. The Americans, further, possessed fine merchant ships but no navy, and they could offer Britain zero resistance at sea.

Why, then, were the Americans victorious? There was, certainly, nothing "inevitable" about their victory. At least twice the revolutionary cause came close to catastrophe. Benedict Arnold's plan to surrender West Point, if successful, might well have blocked the achievement of independence for generations. There was, too, a tremendous element of luck in de Grasse's victory over the British in the indecisive naval engagement of September 5–9, 1781. If de Grasse had suffered severe damage, either through enemy action or storm, he would have sailed away to refit, just as D'Estaing did after the Rhode Island encounter in September 1778. The stalemate would have continued; the success of the revolutionary cause would have been indefinitely delayed.

The American Revolution was a popular struggle; the revolutionary cause enjoyed overwhelming support of large numbers of ordinary people who dedicated their lives to a great ideal and were prepared to die for it. This in itself could not guarantee the final victory of the revolutionaries, but it did mean that the British could never conquer their foes. The British learned through long and costly experience that they might seize strongpoints—islands, coastal towns, and seaports—and that they might enjoy in these enclaves a certain measure of security. But to leave their bases and venture inland was to invite disaster. The militia sprang up to slow the advance and to cut off supply lines; sooner or later there would be, wherever the British went, a Continental force to give inspiration and direction to the popular resistance. As the supply lines lengthened, the hazards increased of being caught, in the most literal sense, off base. From the battle of Lexington in 1775 to Guilford Court House in 1781 this was a simple, unalterable fact of British experience.

The nature, then, of the American cause must be reckoned as a basic factor in the struggle and in the balance of military forces. The fact is, incredible though it seems, that barefoot and ragged Continentals, frightened militia, and children armed with stones prevailed against the greatest empire in the world. This was a people in arms, fighting for their soil, their families, and their homes against a foreign invader.

Another factor that must be reckoned with in explaining the American victory is the sheer physical size of the country. The armies had to traverse vast distances; the continent was so huge that it could absorb with ease, and swallow up, whatever forces were sent against it. The sweeping scale on which operations had to be conducted was, therefore, not a negligible factor in the American victory. How true this is emerges from a comparison with the situation in Ireland; when the American Revolution broke out, the British had been holding down a rebellious Irish population for several centuries. That the British enjoyed the success in Ireland they did was due to the tiny area they had to occupy. And even here the flaming unquenched spirit of popular resistance caused the invader endless trouble.

The final blow to the British was delivered by French sea power. Cornwallis surrendered and the entire British campaign in the South collapsed because the French fleet was in the right place at the right time and was able to prevent British supplies and reinforcements from coming in by sea.

What precisely did the Revolution win for the American nation?

It won, first of all, the independence and sovereignty that had been set forth in the Declaration of Independence as a primary war aim. But the implications of independence became clear neither rapidly nor dramatically. There were few immediate or particularly important changes in the American social structure. The lands of wealthy Tories who had fled the country were confiscated and sold; a number of black people in the North won their freedom from slavery as the reward of military service. But these changes were trivial. The fact that some slaves were freed did not, unfortunately, mean the end of slavery. Throughout the South it remained as firmly entrenched as it had been before the Revolution.

No, the American Revolution was important, not for its immediate impact upon the social structure, but for its ultimate effects. Only in the long run would its meaning become clear. We saw, at the very outset of the Revolution—New York in 1776—the country's first steam engine being put into operation to pump water. In the course of time there would be many more of these engines, and they would be harnessed to the country's developing industrial system to turn its many wheels. Without the American Revolution the gigantic industrialization of the nineteenth century would never have occurred, for Britain valued her colonies as non-industrial, raw-material-producing areas. She had taken steps to limit their overseas trade and to prevent them from developing iron and steel production and manufacturing enterprises of their own. The Revolution swept away the legal barriers to economic development. It made possible a process of economic change that would ultimately transform American society itself. It provided a key for the development of the productive forces that until then were latent, or suppressed.

The revolutionary war resulted in the conquest from Britain of the huge western territories lying between the Appalachians and the Mississippi River. In the years following the Revolution the American people moved westward into these virgin lands, cleared and settled them. In the process their numbers multiplied, and they provided an ever growing market for the manufactured goods of the East. The very pace of American industrial development, therefore, was directly related to the western lands, which were themselves a fruit of the struggle for independence.

The Declaration of Independence enshrined the heritage of the Revolution for the American nation and for mankind. But it was rent by a deep contradiction. It promised freedom and the inalienable rights of man to all. When the smoke of battle cleared, this promise had been realized only for some. So long as men in the United States remained in chains or were treated as second-class citizens, just as long would the Revolution be unfinished, its promises unrealized, its achievement incomplete. This is why the Revolution lives on into our own time wherever men in this country do battle for the rights that are theirs and that have so long been denied them.

Not only in this country, but everywhere in the world today, people are struggling for independence, freedom, and nationhood just as the Americans struggled for it in 1776. The revolutionary heritage of the United States teaches us to honor those who fight for independence and to oppose those who seek to suppress such honorable struggles with fire and sword.

SONG NOTES

Young Ladies in Town
Fairly slow (*andante*). This song first appeared in the *Boston News Letter* in 1769. The melody, provided by Maine folksinger Bill Bonyun, is a variant of "The Miller of Dee." Guitar arrangement by Robert A. and John A. Scott.

The Deserter
With deliberate speed (*moderato*). This great English broadside dates from the middle of the eighteenth century; the melody is provided by a Scots folksinger, Ewan McColl. Guitar arrangement (for advanced students) by Kent Sidon.

The Rich Lady Over the Sea
Swings along with deliberate speed (*moderato*). This revolutionary ballad was collected from the oral tradition and, as far as we know, did not appear in print until 1889. Guitar arrangement by John W. and John A. Scott.

Junto Song
Moderato. This musical satire was first published in the *New York Journal*, September 7, 1775. The melody to which it was set was a Scots beggar song, "A-begging We Will Go." Guitar arrangement by John A. Scott.

Sir Peter Parker

This light-hearted ditty (*allegro*) was widely printed and sung in 1777. The melody—provided by we don't know whom—is a jig tune. Guitar arrangement by John A. Scott and Kent Sidon.

The Dying Redcoat

Slow (*adagio*). This ballad comes down to us from the revolutionary days both through oral tradition and surviving song sheets, or broadsides. The fine melody is provided by Frank Warner, who learned it from an old-time woodsman, Yankee John Galusha of Minerva, New York. The guitar arrangement (for advanced students) is by Kent Sidon.

Ballad of Nathan Hale

Adagio. We have no information about the authorship of this lament, or the date of its composition. The melody, provided by Bill Bonyun, is an adaptation of one used in another, and probably later, Nathan Hale ballad. Guitar arrangement by John A. Scott.

General Burgoyne's Surrender

This cheerful song (*allegro*) is one of many that were written in 1777 to celebrate Burgoyne's defeat or tell of his exploits. The tune to which this one was set—"The Girl I Left Behind Me"—is an old marching song. Guitar accompaniment is not particularly appropriate. The melody is fine for fife or violin. The best accompaniment for voice is probably a single drum.

How Stands the Glass Around?

With a rapid beat (*presto*). Both poignant lament and bitter protest, this seventeenth-century English song was a favorite of General James Wolfe. Guitar arrangement by Robert A. Scott.

Battle of the Kegs
The lyrics of this 1777 song are by Francis Hopkinson; the tune to which it was set is "Yankee Doodle" *(allegro)*. Guitar arrangement by John A. Scott.

Ballad of Major Andre
To be sung lightly, and fairly fast *(allegro)*. This song has come down to us through broadsides published during the Revolution. The melody is provided by John Allison, Hudson Valley song-collector. Guitar arrangement by John A. Scott.

Lord Cornwallis' Surrender
With measured beat *(andante)*. The lyrics, which appeared in contemporary broadsides and newspapers, were set to the tune of the British army's popular "British Grenadier." Guitar arrangement by John A. Scott.

BIBLIOGRAPHY

This bibliography has been designed for the reference of teachers, students, and school librarians; includes the main sources used in the preparation of this book; and offers suggestions for further reading on the various topics. All works listed are in print at the time of writing (1969) unless otherwise stated.

General

Some first-rate documentary sources are available for a study of the revolutionary era. A classic survey of American life at this time is J. Hector St. John Crevecoeur, *Letters from an American Farmer,* based upon some twenty years' life in the colonies, and first published in 1782 (New York: Dutton Everyman paperback, 1967). A number of political pamphlets, indispensable for an understanding of the revolutionary crisis, are available in Merrill Jensen and others, *Tracts of the American Revolution 1773–76* (New York: Bobbs-Merrill, hardcover and paperback, 1967). Jensen's work is to be preferred, in terms of both scale and expense, to Bernard Bailyn's more detailed collection, *Pamphlets of the American Revolution 1750–76* (Cambridge, Mass.: Belknap Press of Harvard University Press, Vol. 1, 1965). Alden T. Vaughan, ed., *Chronicles of the American Revolution Orig-*

inally Compiled by Hezekiah Niles (New York: Grosset and Dunlap Universal Library Original, 1965), is a useful abridgment of a number of important documents brought together by a pioneer compiler. For British sources, see Martin Kallich and Andrew MacLeish, eds., *The American Revolution Through British Eyes* (New York: Harper and Row paperback, 1962), and Elliott R. Barkan, ed., *Edmund Burke on the American Revolution* (New York: Harper Torchbook, 1966).

For the period of the revolutionary wars 1775–1783, a fine introductory selection is provided by Richard Dorson, ed., *America Rebels: Narratives of the Patriots* (New York: Pantheon Books, 1953; Fawcett Premier paperback, 1966). *Eyewitness Accounts of the American Revolution* (New York: Arno Press, 1968) makes available in facsimile many important pamphlets, memoirs, and journals, some of which have been out of print for 150 years or more. These are simply reprints, not critical editions prepared with the needs of a modern audience in mind. An incomparably vivid record of the revolutionary press is available in the compilation of Frank Moore, *The Diary of the American Revolution*, John Anthony Scott, ed. (New York: Washington Square Press, hardcover, 1967; paperback, 1968).

The papers of a number of revolutionary leaders are available in multivolume editions, notably Jefferson's (Princeton University Press), Hamilton's (Columbia University Press), Franklin's (Yale University Press), and John Adams's (Harvard University Press). A portion of this last collection, *The Diary and Autobiography of John Adams*, has been issued as a paperback in four volumes (New York: Athenaeum Press, 1964).

The sources for revolutionary songs are Frank Moore, ed., *Songs and Ballads of the American Revolution* (originally published 1854; reissued by the Kennikat Press, Port Washington, N.Y., 1964); *The Diary of the American Revolution*, cited above; and John Anthony Scott, *The Ballad of America* (New York: Bantam paperback, 1966; Grosset and Dunlap, 1967). *The American Heritage Book of the Revolution* (New York: Simon and Schuster, 1958) contains reproductions of a number of contemporary paintings, drawings, and prints. *The Atlantic Neptune*—a major scientific achievement of the war years, being the Royal Navy's system of charts of the colonial coasts and waterways—has been reissued in five series by Barre Publishers (Barre, Mass., 1967–69).

Turning to the secondary sources, Moses Coit Tyler's *Literary History of the American Revolution* has never been equaled as a survey of literature of the revolutionary era (originally published 1897; reissued in two volumes by Frederick Ungar, New York, 1957). Evarts B. Greene, *The Revolutionary Generation* (New York: Macmillan, 1945), is a picture of American civilization 1763–1790. City life at this time is dealt with in Carl Bridenbaugh's exhaustive *Cities in Revolt: Urban Life in America 1743–76* (New York: Alfred A. Knopf, 1965). John Richard Alden, *The South in the Revolution 1763–89* (Baton Rouge, La.: Louisiana State University Press, 1957), provides a clearly written regional survey. Basic for reference purposes is Lawrence Henry Gipson, *The British Empire Before the American Revolution* (13 vols.; New York: Alfred A. Knopf, 1956–67), in particular Volumes IX to XIII, which cover the period 1763–76.

There are a number of excellent surveys of the military conflict: Willard M. Wallace, *Appeal to Arms* (Chicago: Quadrangle paperback, 1964); John R. Alden, *The American Revolution 1775–83* (New York: Harper and Bros., 1954); and R. Ernest and N. Trevor Dupuy, *The Compact History of the Revolutionary War* (New York: Hawthorn

Books, 1963). George F. Scheer and Hugh F. Rankin, *Rebels and Redcoats* (New York: New American Library Mentor paperback, 1959), draws heavily on eyewitness accounts. Piers Mackesy, *The War for America 1775–83* (Cambridge, Mass.: Harvard University Press, 1964), places the struggle in its imperial perspective. Samuel Flagg Bemis, *The Diplomacy of the American Revolution* (Bloomington, Indiana: University of Indiana Press Midland paperback, 1957), surveys the republic's foreign relations.

Biographical studies are of particular importance in the history of war. Washington, who in this respect falls into a category by himself, is the subject of two major works: Douglas Southall Freeman, *George Washington: A Biography* (7 vols.; New York: Charles Scribner's Sons, 1951), indispensable for reference purposes; and James Thomas Flexner, *George Washington* (2 vols.; Boston: Little, Brown and Co., 1965 and 1967). A useful work on a much smaller scale is Shelby Little, *George Washington 1732–1799* (New York: Capricorn paperback, 1962). Mason L. Weems's myth-making *Life*—with cherries and a hatchet on the cover —has been reissued as a John Harvard Library paperback (Cambridge, Mass.: The Belknap Press of Harvard University Press, 1962), edited by Marcus Cunliffe. Other useful biographies will be mentioned in their appropriate place.

The significance of the American Revolution in the perspective of history is discussed in J. Franklin Jameson, *The American Revolution Considered as a Social Movement* (Boston: Beacon Press, 1956); Dan Lacy, *The Meaning of the American Revolution* (New York: New American Library, 1964); and Richard Morris, *The American Revolution Reconsidered* (New York: Harper Torchbook paperback, 1967).

The status and role of the black man in America at this time is surveyed in Benjamin Quarles, *The Negro in the*

American Revolution (Chapel Hill, N.C.: University of North Carolina Press, 1961), and Arthur Zilversmit, *The First Emancipation: The Abolition of Slavery in the North* (Chicago: University of Chicago Press, 1967).

1 / *The Land of the Grasshoppers*

J. Hector St. John Crevecoeur's *Letters from an American Farmer* (New York: Dutton Everyman paperback, 1967) is a fundamental source for this chapter. Charles Woodmason's *Journal* and other writings are available in Richard J. Hooker, ed., *The Carolina Backcountry on the Eve of the Revolution* (Chapel Hill, N.C.: University of North Carolina Press, 1953). See also Carl Bridenbaugh, *Cities in Revolt: Urban Life in America 1743–76* (New York: Alfred A. Knopf, 1965), and *The Colonial Craftsman* (Chicago: Phoenix paperback, 1961).

2 / *Unlicensed Liberty*

Sources for this period are provided in Merrill Jensen, *Tracts of the American Revolution* (New York: Bobbs-Merrill, 1967), and Edmund S. and Helen M. Morgan, *Prologue to Revolution: Sources and Documents on the Stamp Act Crisis 1764–6* (Chapel Hill, N.C.: University of North Carolina Press paperback, 1959). The text of the Stamp Act is printed in full under that title in Harper's *Encyclopedia of United States History* (New York, 1905). The roots of the new imperial policy and the colonial revolt against it are examined in Charles M. Andrews, *The Colonial Background of the American Revolution* (New Haven: Yale University Press paperback, 1961), and Bernard Knollenberg, *Origins of the American Revolution 1759–66* (New York: Macmillan, 1960). See also Edmund and Helen Morgan, *The Stamp Act Crisis* (Chapel Hill, N.C.:

University of North Carolina Press hardcover, 1953; New York: Collier paperback).

3 / *Shawmut Peninsula*

Materials for the military occupation were drawn from *The Journal of the Times*, compiled by Oliver M. Dickerson under the title *Boston Under Military Rule 1768–9* (Boston: Chapman and Grimes, 1936). This is a limited edition long out of print whose reissue is overdue. For the Boston massacre, see *The Legal Papers of John Adams*, L. Kinvin Wroth and Hiller B. Zobel, eds., Vol. III, *The Boston Massacre Trials* (Cambridge, Mass.: Harvard University Press, 1965). For colonial Boston see Carl Bridenbaugh, *Cities in Revolt: Urban Life in America 1743–76* (New York: Alfred A. Knopf, 1965); Darrett B. Rutman, *Winthrop's Boston* (Chapel Hill, N.C.: University of North Carolina Press, 1965); and Walter Muir Whitehill, *Boston, A Topographical Survey* (Cambridge, Mass.: Belknap Press of Harvard University Press, 1959).

4 / *To Lexington and Back*

The Diary of Frederick Mackenzie, an exceedingly useful and reliable source for the British side not only at Lexington, but throughout the war, was originally published in 1930 and has been reissued in two volumes by Arno Press (New York, 1968). The testimony of Captain John Parker and other militiamen is contained in *A Narrative of the Excursion and Ravages of the King's Troops under the Command of General Gage on the 19th April, 1775* (New York: Arno Press, 1968). For other contemporary reports see Frank Moore, *Diary of the American Revolution*, John Anthony Scott, ed. (New York: Washington Square Press, hardcover, 1967; paperback, 1968). Three monographs very useful for the period here under consideration are Benjamin W.

Labaree, *The Boston Tea Party* (New York. Oxford University Press, 1964); John R. Galvin, *The Minute Men* (New York: Hawthorn Books, 1967); and Arthur B. Tourtellot, *Lexington and Concord: The Beginning of the War of the American Revolution* (Norton Library paperback, 1963).

5 / The Blaze of War

Much interesting and relevant material, including the Earl of Dunmore's proclamation, is available in Frank Moore, *Diary of the American Revolution,* John Anthony Scott, ed. (New York: Washington Square Press, hardcover, 1967; paperback, 1968). Bunker Hill is the subject of a detailed study: *Story of Bunker Hill* by Thomas J. Fleming (New York: Collier paperback, 1962). The loyalists in the war are the subject of Paul H. Smith's path-breaking *Loyalists and Redcoats: A Study in British Revolutionary Policy* (Chapel Hill, N.C.: University of North Carolina Press, 1964). See also William H. Nelson, *The American Tory* (New York: Oxford University Press, 1961; Beacon Press paperback, 1964), and Lorenzo Sabine, *A Historical Essay on the Loyalists of the American Revolution* (Springfield, Mass.: Walden Press, 1957). For the connection between loyalism and bondage, see Richard Morris, *Government and Labor in Early America* (New York: Columbia University Press, 1946); Warren Smith, *White Servitude in Colonial South Carolina* (Columbia, S.C.: University of South Carolina Press, 1961), and Benjamin Quarles, *The Negro in the American Revolution* (Chapel Hill, N.C.: University of North Carolina Press, 1961). The Sullivan's Island episode, which cannot be understood apart from British plans to recruit black slaves and white back-country people, was based primarily upon Thomas Moultrie, *Memoirs of the American Revolution* (New York: Arno Press, 1968).

6 / Independence

Common Sense is available in various paperback editions. Jefferson's original draft of the Declaration of Independence and his *Summary View of the Rights of British America* will be found together in John Anthony Scott, ed., *Living Documents in American History*, Vol. I, *From Earliest Colonial Times to the Civil War* (New York: Washington Square Press, hardcover and paperback, 1964). Jefferson's *Notes on the Proceedings of the Continental Congress* are in his papers (Princeton University Press, Vol. I). The record of Jefferson's own life and correspondence as a slave owner is brought together in Edwin Betts, ed., *Thomas Jefferson's Farm Book* (Charlottesville, Va.: University of Virginia Press, 1951). For press reports on the people's reception of the Declaration of Independence see Frank Moore, *Diary of the American Revolution*, John Anthony Scott, ed. (New York: Washington Square Press, hardcover, 1967; paperback, 1968). A useful guide to the literature on the Declaration is provided by Robert Ginsberg, ed., *A Casebook on the Declaration of Independence* (New York: Thomas Y. Crowell paperback, 1967).

7 / The Trumpet of a Prophecy

Patrick M'Roberts, *A Tour through the North Provinces of America, being a Series of Letters wrote on the Spot in the Years 1774 and 1775*, was originally published in Edinburgh in 1776, and printed in the *Pennsylvania Magazine of History and Biography*, April 1935, with notes by Carl Bridenbaugh. *The Journal of Isaac Bangs, April 1 to July 29, 1776*, edited by Edward Bangs, was originally issued in 1890. *A Brief Narrative of the Ravages of the British and Hessians at Princeton in 1776–7*, Varnum L. Collins, ed., was originally published in 1906. All three pamphlets have been reissued by Arno Press (New York, 1968). Other major sources for this chapter were Frank Moore, *Diary of the American Revolution*, John Anthony Scott, ed. (New York: Washington Square Press, hardcover, 1967; paperback 1968); and *The Diary of Frederick Mackenzie* (2 vols.; New York: Arno Press, 1968). Thomas Paine's "Crisis Papers" are reproduced in *Common Sense and Crisis* (New York: Doubleday Dolphin paperback, no date). The fundamental secondary source for Washington's counterattack across the Delaware is Alfred Hoyt Bill, *The Campaign of Princeton 1776–77* (Princeton, N.J.: Princeton University Press, 1948).

8 / *The Nether Millstone*

Information about American military prisoners in New York and elsewhere is provided in Ethan Allen, *Narrative of Colonel Ethan Allen's Captivity* (New York: Corinth Books, 1961); in *The Diary of Frederick Mackenzie*, Vol. I (New York: Arno Press, 1968); in Frank Moore, *Diary of the American Revolution*, John Anthony Scott, ed. (New York: Washington Square Press, hardcover, 1967; paperback, 1968); and in John Joseph Henry, *Account of Arnold's Campaign Against Quebec* (New York: Arno Press, 1968). Two journals that tell the experiences of British prisoners in American hands are *The Diary of Lt. Anthony Allaire* and *Lt. James Moody's Narrative of his Exertions and Sufferings* (both, New York: Arno Press, 1968).

For the story of captive seamen, see Thomas Dring, *Recollections of the Jersey Prison-Ship* (New York: Corinth Books paperback, 1961). *The Adventures of Christopher Hawkins* (New York: Arno Press, 1968) tells the experience of a man who escaped from the *Jersey*. Portions of the story of Thomas Andros, another *Jersey* prisoner, are reproduced in Richard Dorson, ed., *America Rebels: Narratives of the Patriots* (New York: Pantheon Books, 1953; Fawcett Premier paperback, 1966).

9 / *The Cannon and the Drums*

Much original and interesting documentation will be found in Frank Moore, *Diary of the American Revolution*, John Anthony Scott, ed. (New York: Washington Square Press, hardcover, 1967; paperback, 1968), notably Burgoyne's proclamation and Hopkinson's reply, the story of General Prescott's capture, Gates's letter of October 20 to his wife, and some of the songs commemorating the surrender. See also Roger Lamb, *An Original and Authentic Journal of Occurences during the Late American War* (New York: Arno Press, 1968); and the Marquis de Chastellux, *Travels in North America*, Howard C. Rice, Jr., ed. (2 vols.; Raleigh, N.C.: University of North Carolina Press, 1963). The Rhode Island coup is also vividly covered in *The Diary of Frederick Mackenzie*, Vol. I (New York: Arno Press, 1968). The definitive edition of Mme. Riedesel's journal is *Baroness von Riedesel and the American Revolution*, Marvin L. Brown, Jr., ed. and trans. (Chapel Hill, N.C.: University of North Carolina Press, 1965). There are two studies of Burgoyne's campaign: John R. Cuneo, *The Battles of Saratoga* (New York: Macmillan, 1967), excellently illustrated and with clear battle plans; and Harrison Bird, *March to Sarotoga: General Burgoyne and the American Campaign, 1777* (New York: Oxford University Press, 1963). Allan Valentine, *Lord George Germain* (New York: Oxford University Press, 1962), is a helpful biography that cites important correspondence in the imperial files.

10 / *The Cold Ground*

Valuable documentation for this chapter is to be found in Frank Moore, *Diary of the American Revolution*, John Anthony Scott, ed. (New York: Washington Square Press, hardcover, 1967; paperback, 1968). *Major Andre's Journal: Opera-*

tions of the British Army under Lieutenant Generals Sir William Howe and Sir Henry Clinton, June 1777-1778, was published in 1930 and is available as a reprint (New York: Arno Press, 1968). Joseph Plumb Martin, *A Narrative of Some of the Adventures, Dangers, and Sufferings of a Revolutionary Soldier*, is available in two modern editions: (1) *Private Yankee Doodle, Being a Narrative of Some of the Adventures, Dangers, and Sufferings of a Revolutionary Soldier*, George F. Scheer, ed. (Boston: Little, Brown and Co., 1962; New York: Popular Library paperback, 1963). This is a complete and well-prepared edition of the original *Narrative*. (2) *Yankee Doodle Boy, A Young Soldier's Adventures in the American Revolution Told by Himself*, George F. Scheer, ed. (New York: William R. Scott, 1964). This edition is heavily abridged.

11 / Dark Day

Rich material on the French alliance, the 1778 invasion of Newport, and the military stalemate is provided in Frank Moore, *Diary of the American Revolution*, John Anthony Scott, ed. (New York: Washington Square Press, hardcover, 1967; paperback, 1968). See also *The Diary of Frederick Mackenzie* (2 vols.; New York: Arno Press, 1968). John Joseph Henry, *An Account of Arnold's Campaign Against Quebec* (New York: Arno Press, 1968), is a fine contemporary picture of Arnold's earliest military feat. For Arnold, see also Carl Van Doren, *Secret History of the American Revolution* (New York: Viking Press paperback, 1968).

12 / The Bonny Bunch of Roses

The principal source of this chapter was the *Revolutionary Journal of Baron Ludwig Von Closen*, Evelyn M. Acomb, ed. and trans. (Chapel Hill, N.C.: University of North Carolina Press, 1958). See Joseph Martin's *Narrative* cited in bibliography for Chapter 10; and Frank Moore, *Diary of the American Revolution*, John Anthony Scott, ed. (New York: Washington Square Press, hardcover, 1967; paperback, 1968); and, for the British reaction to the inconclusive naval encounter of September 5 and the following days, *The Diary of Frederick Mackenzie*, Vol. II (New York: Arno Press, 1968). The following biographies deal with some of the people encountered in this chapter: Theodore Thayer, *Nathanael Greene* (New York: Twayne Publishers, 1960); Arnold Whitridge, *Rochambeau* (New York: Macmillan, 1964); and Alice Noble Waring, *The Fighting Elder: Andrew Pickens* (Columbia, S.C.: University of South Carolina Press, 1962). There are two detailed studies of the Yorktown campaign: Donald Barr Chidsey, *Victory at Yorktown* (New York: Crown Publishers, 1962), and Thomas J. Fleming, *Beat the Last Drum* (New York: St. Martin's Press, 1963).

ACKNOWLEDGMENTS

My editors at Knopf have offered assistance and enthusiasm in the preparation of this book. Kent Sidon made an extraordinary contribution as leader of the team that developed guitar arrangements for the revolutionary songs. Mrs. Elizabeth Urbanowicz prepared manuscript drafts with speed and precision. Miss Mary Dilg was of great help in securing pictures.

Grateful acknowledgment is made for the use of illustrations:
Abby Aldrich Rockefeller Folk Art Collection, 244, 270; American Antiquarian Society, *jacket* (courtesy American Heritage), 224, 272; *Baroness and the General,* Louise H. Tharp, Little, Brown and Co., 198; Brown University, 252; Chicago Historical Society, 99; Detroit Institute of Arts, 276; *Diary of the American Revolution,* 181, 210; *Early New England Gravestone Rubbing,* Edmund V. Gillon, reprinted through permission of the publisher, Dover Publications, Inc., *frontis,* 44, 283; Essex Institute, Salem, Mass., 83; Frick Art Reference Library, collection of Fordham University, 174; Historical Society of Pennsylvania, 220; *History of Playing Cards,* Catherine Perry Hargrave, 141; Library of Congress, 88–89, 258; Maritime Museum "Prins Hendrik," 25; Maryland Historical Society, 14;

New-York Historical Society, 67, 129, 134, 149; New York Public Library, 109; New York State Historical Assoc., 191; Philadelphia Museum of Art, 151, 125, 231; Providence Rhode Island Historical Society, Anne S.K. Brown Military Collection, 99; Smithsonian Institution, 11, 143; University of London, Courtauld Institute, 78; Washington & Lee University, 206; West Point Museum Collections, U.S. Army photograph, 61; Yale University Art Gallery, 97. The maps in this book are by John Bierhorst.

INDEX

ception of, 127-129; *see Jefferson, Thomas*
de Grasse, Admiral, 263-265, 279
Delaware River, 154, 157, 205, 211, 215-216, 222-223, 232, 261, 265
Demonstrations, 32, 33-35, 38, 87; *see also Stamp Act; Boston Tea Party*
"Deserter, The," song, 54-55
D'Estaing, Vice Admiral Charles Hector, Comte de, 236, 238-239, 241, 279
Draft, illegal in England, 98; impressment, 51
Dring, Captain Thomas, 170-177; quoted, 170-171, 172-173, 175
Dunmore, Earl of, Governor, 72, 100, 102, 106
"Dying Redcoat, The," song, 144-147

East India Company, 63-64, 65, 70, 71
Edward, Fort, 189, 190, 194, 196

Farmers, 4, 8, 150; *see also Plunder*
Farming, 20, 43, 218
Flogging, 52-56, 77, 211
Food, foraged, 156-157, 182, 209, 211, 218-220; of prisoners of war, 162, 164, 166-167, 171, 173; provisions of armies, 215, 216, 279; *see also Hunger*
France, 3, 19, 20, 22, 205, 268; colonists' alliance with, 228-230, 234-235
Franklin, Benjamin, 74, 116, 121
Freeman's Journal, quoted, 138, 142, 151, 158, 165-166, 168, 169
French army, 257, 262, 269; *see also Rochambeau, Gen.*
French fleet, 230, 234, 236, 237-239, 257, 263, 264, 266, 268, 281
Frontier, 9, 10-12, 17
Frontiersmen, 9, 15; as soldiers, 87, 90-91
Fur trade, 20, 21, 75

Gage, General Sir Thomas, 71-72, 76, 77, 79, 84, 93
Gates, General Horatio, 195, 196, 199, 201, quoted, 201
"General Burgoyne's Surrender," song, 202-203
George III, King, 21, 22, 33, 64, 76, 124, 180, 184, 203, 256, 275; quoted, 21-22; statue of, 133, 140
Georgia, 4, 35, 128, 242, 243
Gerard, Monsieur Louis, 234-236, 240
Germain, Lord George, 93, 98, 142, 179
Germantown, Pa., 215, 228
Government, provincial, 13, 30, 31, 40; Massachusetts, 39, 79; South Carolina, 104; Virginia, 72-73
Greene, General Nathanael, 237, 261, 275
Guerrilla warfare, 82-84, 158-159, 185, 260, 261

Hale, Nathan, 150-153; quoted, 151; song about, 152-153
Hancock, John, 38, 64, 237, 240
Henry, Patrick, 29-30, 72; quoted, 30-31
Hessians, 98, 100, 138, 156-157, 167, 169, 207, 209, 211, 233, 245, 274, 275
Hopkinson, Francis, 183, 184, 223; quoted, 183-184, 224-228
"How Stands the Glass Around?" song, 213-215

102, 104, 108, 111, 129, 155, 159, 164, 185, 238, 239, 248, 250, 261, 279, 280; against Burgoyne, 195-200; at Lexington, 80-81; Col. Barton's, 186-188; in New York, 131, 133, 143, 148-150; in Vermont, 190, 192; system, 76-77; see also Moultrie, Col.

Mississippi Valley, 3, 21, 228

Moultrie, Colonel William, 104, 106, 107, 108, 110; quoted, 104, 106, 107, 108

Moultrie, Fort, 107, 108, 110-111, 163, 248

M'Robert, Patrick, quoted, 130-131, 135, 137

Nantucket, 16, 17

Narragansett Bay, 103, 185, 186, 236, 238-239, 261

New England, 16, 38, 71, 76, 103, 131, 155, 170, 179, 192, 195, 201, 215, 236, 249, 262

New Hampshire, 35, 192, 195

New Jersey, 121, 127, 130, 154, 156, 158, 178, 185, 190, 204, 216, 232, 242, 246, 247, 250, 260; Hessians in, 207-209; Rochambeau in, 264-265

Newport, R. I., 34, 45, 128, 155, 186, 236-239, 257, 263, 264

Newspapers, 23, 26, 27, 34-35

New York, 5, 31, 34, 36, 65, 67, 86, 92, 101, 108, 121, 164, 165, 168, 178, 195, 246, 247, 249, 256, 264; see also New York City

New York City, 128, 170, 177, 179, 190, 204, 230, 232, 236, 238, 248, 250, 262-264, 266, 282; British attack, 130-155; water supply, 135-137; see also Bangs, Lt.; Manhattan

New York Gazette, 238; quoted, 147-148, 239, 246

New York Journal, quoted, 40-42, 229, 234-235, 245

Norfolk, Va., 100, 102

North, Lord, 74, 76

North Carolina, 108, 164, 178, 257, 260

Paine, Thomas, 116-119, 157, 183; quoted, 117, 118-120, 157; see also Common Sense

Parker, Admiral Sir Peter, 108, 111, 163; song about, 112-114

Pennsylvania, 74, 87, 101, 116, 121, 154, 155, 205, 218, 242; see also Philadelphia

Pennsylvania Evening Post, quoted, 102, 127, 128-129, 186, 188, 190, 192

Pennsylvania Journal, 90; quoted, 90-91, 101-102, 140, 142

Philadelphia, 5, 6, 34, 65, 67, 87, 92, 116, 117, 127, 179, 180, 183, 205, 207, 234, 250, 265; British in, 209-212, 220, 222-232; pop. of, 6, 211

Plantations, 13, 15, 22, 27, 108

Plunder, 156-157, 192, 207, 209, 211, 233, 242, 247; see also Food

Population, Boston, 6, 39; British America, 4, 5, 6; Charleston, 13; Colonial, 20; Manhattan, 6, 137; Philadelphia, 211

Poverty, 4, 9, 10, 11, 98; see also Immigrants

Prescott, General Richard, 185-186, 188, 201, 260

Princeton, N.J., 169, 233

Prisoners of war, 160-177

Protests, 13, 53-55; see also Demonstrations

Quebec, 90, 93, 132, 250

Radicalization, 31, 103-104, 115-116, 156
Regulators, 13, 106, 108
Religion, 9-12, 18, 49-51, 137, 229-230
Resistance movements, 42-43, 73, 74, 76, 246, 280; against tea tax, 65, 67; armed, 77, 79; Lexington, 82; revolutionary conventions, 86, 120-122, 131
Rhode Island, 34, 128, 155, 170, 178, 185, 201, 230, 236-239; French at, 257, 259, 260, 262, 266, 279
"Rich Lady Over the Sea, The," song, 68-70
Riedesel, Baroness Frederika, quoted, 194-195, 196, 197, 200, 201
Rifles, 90-91; rifle companies, 87, 90
Rivington's Gazette, quoted, 212, 240-241, 245
Rochambeau, Marquis de, 257, 262-264, 265, 269, 277

Saratoga, N.Y., 90, 132, 203; battle of, 195-200
Seamen, 5, 16-18, 66, 75; English, 110, 177; pilots, 29; *see also* Prisoners of war
Shawmut Peninsula, 38, 39, 131
Shippen, Peggy, 232, 250
"Sir Peter Parker," song, 112-114
Slavery, 13-15, 106, 123-124, 126, 176, 281; *see also* Jefferson, Thomas
Slaves, 4, 13-15, 33, 56, 60, 93, 106, 123-126, 150, 176, 243, 247, 277; Andrew, 59-60; emancipation of, 101-102, 106-107; in New York, 137; runaway, 101-102, 108

Smuggling, 64-65
Songs, 46, 54, 68, 85, 94, 112, 144, 152, 202, 213, 221, 224, 240, 253, 272
Sons of Liberty, 31, 32, 36, 140
South Carolina, 9, 10, 13, 104, 138, 163, 178, 248, 257, 260; Provincial Congress of, 104; *see also* Charleston
Stamp Act, 23-24, 26-27, 30, 31, 32, 36, 37; quoted, 24, 26; repealed, 36; resistance to, 30-36
Staten Island, 130, 138, 178, 204, 247
Steam engine, 136-137, 282
Steuben, Baron Frederick von, 220, 222
Taxes, 23, 27, 30, 31, 36, 55, 63, 67; on tea, 63-64, 68-70; Townshend Duties, 37-42; *see also* Stamp Act
Tea, 64, 65, 66-67, 71; tax on, 63-64, 68-70; *see also* Boston Tea Party
Terrorism, 156-157, 182-183, 242-248; British naval, 102-103
Ticonderoga, Fort, 131, 180, 183, 184, 189, 203, 250
Tories, *see* Loyalists
Townshend Duties, 37, 42, 63; *see also* Taxes
Trenton, N.J., 157, 158, 169
Trinity Church, N.Y.C., 148
Tyranny, British, 49, 73, 76, 117, 119, 123, 157

Underdeveloped country, 4, 18, 282

Valley Forge, 205, 212-215, 216-220, 222, 223, 229, 230, 246
Vermont, 131, 192, 195
Virginia, 27, 72, 73, 86, 87, 90, 92, 93, 101, 102, 120, 121, 235,

JOHN ANTHONY SCOTT, author of *Trumpet of a Prophecy* and general editor of *The Living History Library*, was born in London, England, in 1916. He was educated at Oxford and received his Ph.D. from Columbia University. He has taught students at every level from junior high school to graduate—at Columbia University, Amherst College, Rutgers University School of Law, and the Fieldston School in Riverdale, New York.

Among the books Professor Scott has authored or edited are *The Ballad of America, Living Documents in American History, Settlers on the Eastern Shore 1607–1750*, Frances A. Kemble's *Journal of a Residence on a Georgian Plantation in 1838–1839*, and *The Defense of Gracchus Babeuf before the High Court of Vendôme*.

The text of this book is set in the type face called Electra
Composed by Brown Bros. Linotypers, New York City
Printed by Halliday Lithograph Corp., West Hanover, Mass.
Bound by The Book Press, Brattleboro, Vt.